THE CUNARD STORY

HOWARD JOHNSON
CUNARD STORY

Whittet Books

(*Title page*) The Cunard
fleet in the late 1950s;
beginning at the front, from
left to right, *Mauretania*
(II), *Caronia, Saxonia,
Ivernia, Andrea, Carinthia,
Sylvania, Britannic, Medea,
Parthea, Queen Elizabeth,
Queen Mary, Franconia,
Alsatia, Ascania, Scythia,
Assyria, Asia, Arabia,
Brescia, Lycia, Phrygia* and
Pavia.

First published 1987
© 1987 by Howard Johnson
Whittet Books Ltd, 18 Anley Road, London W14 0BY

Design by Richard Kelly

British Library Cataloguing in Publication Data

Johnson, Howard
  The Cunard story.
  1. Cunard Line —— History
  I. Title
  387.5′065′41   HE945.C9

ISBN 0−905483−57−X

The author and publishers are most grateful to the following for permission to
reproduce photographs that appear on the pages quoted in brackets after their names:
Australian War Memorial (p. 160(2)); Philip Bates (p. 145); Cunard (pp. 160, 186, 194);
Cunard Line, New York (p. 156); Cunard Archives, University of Liverpool (pp. 10, 15, 19,
23, 24, 26, 29, 32, 34, 35, 38, 39, 43, 44, 50, 51, 53, 56, 59(2), 61, 62, 64(3), 70, 77, 78(top), 92,
99 (bottom), 100, 103, 104, 107, 110, 111, 112, 113, 115, 118, 121, 123, 126, 127, 132, 140(2),
142, 145(2), 146(2), 154, 166, 167, 170, 172, 173, 174, 178, 181); *Financial Times* (p. 160);
Illustrated London News (p. 100); Imperial War Museum (pp. 28, 30, 42, 43(bottom),
49(2), 52, 57(2), 58, 59(bottom), 60, 68, 69(2), 72, 75, 78(bottom), 79(2), 82); Commodore
Geoffrey Marr, D.S.C. (p. 165); Mary Evans Picture Library (pp. 9, 46(2), 47, 48, 64); The
National Maritime Museum, London (pp. 28, 30, 42, 43(bottom), 49(2), 52, 57(2), 58,
59(bottom), 60, 68, 69(2), 72, 75, 78(bottom), 79(2), 82); New York Port Authority
(p. 82); Photoflex (p. 156); Southampton Maritime Museums (pp. 64, 67(4), 80, 91, 97, 98,
99(top), 103(6)).

Typeset by Inforum Ltd, Portsmouth
Printed and bound by South China Printing Co., Hong Kong

Contents

Acknowledgments

The author and publishers wish to express their grateful thanks to the following for assistance, advice and encouragement in the writing and production of *The Cunard Story*:

Mr and Mrs Philip Bates, Mr W.B. Slater, C.B.E., and Mr Brian Barlow (Company Secretary of the Cunard Steam-Ship Company), all of whom have guided the author and produced valuable sources of information throughout the research and writing of this book; Mr Ralph Bahna (Managing Director of the Cunard Passenger Shipping and Hotels Division); Mr A.J. MacIntosh (Managing Director of the Cunard Cargo and Aviation Division), Mr J.G. Dalton and Mr G. Law of Cunard; Mr Derek Hollebone, M.B.E., M.C., and Mr Eric Sutton of Port Line; Miss Susan Alpert (Public Relations Manager, Cunard, New York); Miss Alice Marshall (former Manager, Public Relations, New York); Miss Anne Bright (Cunard Office, Pall Mall); Miss Andrea D. Rudd (Secretary to the Liverpool University archivist); Mr N. Windle (Manager, office personnel, Cunard, Southampton); Mr Nigel Overton (Keeper of Maritime History, Department of Leisure Services, Southampton); Mr M.K. Stammers (Assistant Director, Liverpool Maritime Museum); Sir Charles Baring; Mr William Tanner; Mr Nicholas Hayward (of the Seaview Hotel, Seaview, Isle of Wight); and former officers and crew members of Cunard ships.

The author further wishes to acknowledge that in researching and preparing the story of the life of the founder of the Cunard Line, Sir Samuel Cunard, and the financial management of the company over the years, it has been necessary to be guided by previously published sources. The books, *Samuel Cunard, Pioneer of the Atlantic Steamship* by Kay Grant (Abelard-Schuman, London, New York and Toronto, 1967) and *Cunard and the North Atlantic* by the late Professor Francis E. Hyde (Macmillan Press Ltd, 1975), were especially helpful. Thanks also go to Alastair Forsyth, author of the forthcoming book, *Art and Design on the Greatest British Liners*.

The author and publishers are also grateful to Mr Peter Knight for permission to reprint an extract from the diary of Henry Knight; to Angus and Robertson for permission to reprint the extract from *Commodore, War, Peace and Big Ships* by Sir James Bisset in collaboration with P.R. Stephenson; to Leo Cooper (publishers) and Watson, Little Limited (licensing agents) for permission to reprint the extract from *Armed Merchant Cruisers* by Kenneth Poolman; and to A.D. Peters for the extract from Laurie Lee.

Foreword

Many books have been written about Cunard, all of which have contributed in no small way in ensuring that the history of the Company is recorded for all time.

In this particular book, *The Cunard Story*, Howard Johnson has gone to considerable lengths to describe the early days of Samuel Cunard and has then, in his own inimitable manner, so aptly covered the period up to the present day, emphasizing the affinity between the past and the future and identifying the courage, determination and perception of those concerned, which has seen Cunard through almost one hundred and fifty exciting years as a major force in world shipping.

It is of particular interest to record that in 1987 we will be commemorating the bicentenary of the birth of Sir Samuel Cunard, whose life was devoted to the formation of the company which bears his name, and will be welcoming back into service our flagship, the *Queen Elizabeth 2*, after an extended refit and re-engining.

As explained by Howard Johnson, the *Queen Elizabeth 2*, together with the container ships which have very largely replaced the conventional cargo fleet, are ample evidence that Cunard is maintaining the great traditions of the past and consequently I would recommend this book to you.

Eric W. Parker
Group Chief Executive
Trafalgar House Public Limited Company
Chairman of the Cunard Steam-Ship Company p.l.c.

'A ship was cynically defined by Dr Johnson as "a prison, with the chance of being drowned".

'But of Cunard it may be assuredly said that it is a cheerful, hospitable and elegant floating hotel, with the certainty, personally speaking, of reaching your journey's end in safety.'

GEORGE AUGUSTUS SALA
(Travel writer and journalist, 1828–95)

PART ONE

1840-1900

Britannia leaving Liverpool
on July 4th, 1840. An artist
captures the great moment
when Cunard's first
transatlantic mail paddle
steamer sails for America.

(*Previous page*) Britannia
trapped in the ice at Boston
in 1844. Hundreds of men
and horses worked day and
night to cut her free.

CHAPTER·ONE

In Pursuit of a Dream

Nearly a century and a half ago, the first Cunarder, the wooden paddle-steamer *Britannia*, swung out from the Coburg Dock at Liverpool at the start of her pioneering maiden voyage to Nova Scotia and America. She was carrying 63 passengers, 93 crew members and bags of Her Majesty's mail for Halifax and Boston, inaugurating the first regular Atlantic mail service by steamer.

It was high tide at Liverpool on the evening of Saturday, July 4th, 1840, the anniversary of American Independence, and the crowds that lined the dockside gave three cheers as the master, Captain Woodruff, R.N., standing on the paddle-box, shouted his orders to the crew through a speaking trumpet, and the huge paddle wheels began to thresh the murky waters of the Mersey. The *Britannia* was hardly the most elegant of ships, nevertheless she was indisputably one of the most functional of her day. A two-decker with one tall orange-red funnel amidships, she was 207 feet long, of 1,145 tons, and coal powered from three furnaces fed from 600 tons of coal. At times the ship required four sailors to man the wheel, depending on the state of the sea, for in rough weather a sailor could be badly injured if 'thrown'.

Britannia was bark-rigged, fore-and-aft rigged on the mizzenmast, square-rigged on the mainmast and foremast. She had a square stern and a clipper bow, with the bronze figurehead of Britannia under the bowsprit. The officers' quarters were on the upper deck, with the galley, bakery and the cowhouse. The cow was to supply fresh milk during the 14-day and 8-hour passage to Boston across the hazardous North Atlantic. The passenger cabins and dining saloon were on the second deck. The cabins had two bunks and only measured eight by six feet. Furniture consisted of a hard settee and a commode with two wash basins, two water jugs and two chamber pots. The saloon contained no luxury items.

The only light in the cabins was a hurricane candle beside the porthole. Candles in the alleyways, suspended in trays, had to be extinguished at ten o'clock each night as a fire precaution. Bed linen was changed on the eighth day of the voyage; towels changed every other day; state rooms swept every morning.

Rules and regulations concerning the behaviour of passengers and crew were posted up on the ship for everyone to read. These included:

— In case of dissatisfaction with any of the servants, it is requested that the Head Steward may be informed, and, if the grievance be not immediately redressed, that the Captain be appealed to, and, if of a serious nature, that it be represented in writing in order that it may be brought before the Agents at the conclusion of the Voyage.

   — The stewards and boys are engaged on the express understanding that at Table they attend in becoming apparel.

   — The state-rooms to be swept, and carpets taken out and shaken, every morning after breakfast. To be washed once a week, if the weather is dry.

   — The saloon and ladies' cabins to be swept every morning before breakfast, beginning at five o'clock.

   — Bedding to be turned over as soon as passengers quit their cabins. Slops to be emptied and basins cleaned at the same time. Beds to be made once a day only, except in cases of illness, etc., and within one hour after breakfast.

   — Passengers are requested not to open their scuttles [portholes] when there is a chance of their bedding being wetted.

   — The stewardess only is to enter the ladies' cabins and state-rooms, and to make the beds at the time before stated.

   — The Wine and Spirit Bar will be opened to passengers at 6 a.m., and closed at 11 p.m.

Amongst the Cunard archives is a personal account of *Britannia*'s first voyage in the form of a letter written by a son to his father when the ship berthed at Boston. Addressed from the Bristol Hotel, Boston, and dated July 19th, 1840, the letter reads:

Dear Father
   As you know I have been asked to go to Boston to appoint new stevedores and was resigned to sailing by packet boat.
   Over breakfast an advertisement in the *LIVERPOOL MERCURY* caught my eye. It said:
   'British and North American Royal Mail Steamship Co. Steamers of 1,200 tons and 440 horse power each. Appointed by the Admiralty to sail for Boston, calling at Halifax, to land passengers and Her Majesty's mails.
Britannia, Captain Henry Woodruff
Acadia, Captain Edward C. Miller
Caledonia, Captain Richard Cleland
Columbia, building.
   'The *Britannia* will sail from Liverpool on the 4th July; the *Acadia* on the 4th August.
   'Passage, including provisions and wine, to Halifax, 34 guineas; to Boston, 38 guineas. Steward's fee: 1 guinea.'

The address of the Liverpool agent was given as D. and C. MacIver, 12 Water Street. My heart leapt. A steamer service at last. What a chance.

Abandoning further food I donned my coat and top hat, hailed a brougham and with it still short of eight set off at a fine trot. My passage booked, the agent, Mr. Charles MacIver himself, informed me that *Britannia* would leave Coburg Dock on Friday, July 3rd and all heavy baggage should be delivered to the dockside by 3 p.m. and that I must attend to clear Customs.

All was done as bidden and in plenty of time I joined the sixty-two other passengers – which included a Mr Samuel Cunard who, I am reliably informed, is the Principal of the company. A Newfoundlander by birth he is of commanding presence with wavy grey hair and modest sideburns. Miss Cunard, who was with him, I found to be a shy and retiring person with a delicate laugh and only the slightest Canadian accent.

It took but an hour to board us all with our somewhat voluminous amounts of hand baggage.

The deck itself was almost impassable being strewn and stacked with cabin trunks and crates of perishable food. Amidships in her padded pen the ship's cow bellowed her disapproval of all this activity. We had gained the deck adjacent to the Purser's office and were there thus greeted individually and had our passports checked. Above us on the port paddle box our commander Captain Woodruff was shouting instructions, through his speaking trumpet, to ensure all haste in boarding the mails, since the company's contract with the Admiralty contained penalties for late sailings.

I noticed, too, the presence of a stewardess for the benefit of the ladies. A white jacketed steward conveyed me on deck down to my stateroom which I found to be very small and totally without any space to stow my modest cabin trunk. The bunk was beneath a square porthole through which I could watch the sea. Beneath the bunk were three drawers for clothing and at the bed head a stand with a jug and wash basin plus chamber commode with fitted lid. Upon enquiry I was told that the water closets themselves were on deck at the forward end of each paddle box – furthermore they were reachable only by recourse to the open deck; this, I thought, did not augur well in stormy seas.

The deck saloon contained two parallel green baize tables which ran the length of the room. Between them were a pair of long benches. Outboard of each table was fixed a continuous leather covered settee. Here we were to pass the day as best we might. Card playing or reading is the main occupation although I noticed that the ladies preferred knitting or sewing.

At meal times the tables are covered with an oil cloth. This I found to be slippery and in practice full plates tended to slip off into one's lap whenever *Britannia* rolled – which she did incessantly. The amount of crockery smashed must be of alarm to the owners. I lost count of the number of times that a sharp roll caused the sound of a cascading clatter of breaking china from the pantry next door.

The food is no advance on that in sail and this disappointed me. The galley, just before the funnel, is no better than in my uncle's ships. Indeed, since the food is carried over open decks it is sometimes cold despite the silver covers. As usual we have fresh food for the first three days and thereafter the fish and meat is salted. *Britannia* has two ice rooms and the fruit is stored there. At least we are sure of avoiding scurvy!

During the voyage I counted pea soup nine times and the ubiquitous Sea Pie was on the menu every day.

Captain Woodruff and the officers joined us for all meals, except breakfast. He is responsible as 'Providore' for the food and used our victualling allowance well. If anything he exceeded the allowance per passenger for each meal which was posted in a wooden frame within the saloon.

You will be amused to know that these Royal Mail steamers are obliged to have at least one cat. We have three. Rats, it seems, like to nibble the hide mail bags and are prone to destroy letters. Our ship has rat proof canvas oakum bags which I am informed are now being made at Her Majesty's Prisons. Nevertheless the cats are always busy as we are forbidden to feed them.

Wooden ships of course need to have their timbers kept wet and sweet. With steam engines there is a tendency for the fires to dry out the wood. Certainly this ship creaks more than I am used to. This leads to the daily hosing down of the decks and engine room side planking. The Chief Engineer told me that even so the ship will sag amidships in a year or two. He also said dry rot is commoner in steam than sail.

Another thing that will surprise you is that after we left Queenstown all the carpets and settee brocades were removed. I soon found out why – once the vessel commenced to roll the sea finds its way down to the stateroom level, and corridors as well as cabins are literally awash. Also those suffering from mal-de-mer are less able to taint the finery once it is stored. My steward deals with these poor wretches by giving them brandy and water and only hard tack biscuits to eat. He is ever attentive; at a doleful bidding from the dark interior of some cabin his cry of, 'What number sir, or madam?' is a familiar sound.

Britannia has a day room for the use of all ladies. To my surprise there are four berths which are booked by single ladies. They are obliged between 9 a.m. and 9 p.m. to host any lady who has a mind to use the room.

But enough about life at sea in this year 1840. We made Halifax after twelve days and ten hours. The vessel remained in port, a hive of activity, for eight hours and then to Boston in the net time of two weeks and eight hours. Here we received an enormous welcome of which I will tell you more in my next letter.

The spartan cabin used by Charles Dickens and his wife in *Britannia*.

Let me end by adding that despite the spartan aspects of the voyage the saving of time and the reliability of arrival augurs well for steam propelled trans-Atlantic vessels.

Your affectionate son John

The spartan life aboard Britannia prompted one famous passenger, Charles Dickens, who took passage to Boston in her on January 3rd, 1842, to describe his dismay on first setting eyes on the gloomy saloon. Dickens, then a man of thirty, who had just published *The Old Curiosity Shop* and was going on an American tour, wrote:

It was a long narrow apartment like a gigantic hearse with windows in the sides; having at the upper end a melancholy stove, at which three or four chilly stewards were warming their hands; while on either side, extending down its whole dreary length, was a long, low table over which a rack, fixed to the low roof, and stuck full of drinking glasses and cruet stands, hinted dismally at rolling seas and heavy weather.

The scene aboard *Britannia* before she sailed was described by Dickens:

The packet is beset by its late freight (passengers) who instantly pervade the whole ship, and are to be met with by the dozen in every nook and corner; swarming down below with their own baggage, and stumbling over other people's; disposing themselves comfortably in wrong cabins, and creating a most horrible confusion by having to turn out again; madly bent on opening locked doors, and in forcing a passage into all kinds of out-of-the-way places where there is no thoroughfare; sending wild stewards, with elfin hair, to and fro upon the breezy decks on unintelligible errands, impossible of execution; and, in short, creating the most extraordinary and bewildering tumult.

Dickens then experienced a two-hour wait for the mail-bags to arrive and explained:

This waiting for the latest mail bags is worse than all . . . to lie here two hours or more, in the damp fog, neither staying at home or going abroad, is letting one gradually down into the very depths of dullness and low spirits. A speck in the mist, at last! That's something. It is the boat we wait for! The Captain appears on the paddle-box with his speaking trumpet; the officers take their stations; all hands are on the alert; the flagging hopes of passengers revive; the cooks pause in their savoury work, and look out with faces full of interest. The boat comes alongside; the bags are dragged in anyhow, and flung down for the moment anywhere. Three cheers more, and, as the first one rings upon our ears, the vessel throbs like a strong giant that has just received the breath of life; the two great wheels turn fiercely round for the first time; and the whole ship, with wind and tide astern, breaks proudly through the lash and foaming water.

Dickens's account of meals in the early Cunarder did not exactly encourage the gourmet to rush from his cabin at the sound of the lunch and dinner bells. The lunch bell would be rung at one o'clock and in came a stewardess with steaming plates of baked potatoes and roasted apples, another steaming dish of hot collops, and an array of cold dishes, salt beef, cold ham and pig's head. The next meal was at five o'clock, this with boiled potatoes, and various hot meats including roast pig 'for medical reasons'.

'We sit down at table again,' wrote Dickens, 'and prolonged the meal with a rather mouldy desert of apples, grapes, and oranges; and drink our wine, and brandy-and-water. The bottles and glasses are still upon the table, and the oranges and so forth are rolling about according to their fancy and the ship's way, when the doctor comes down, by special nightly invitation, to join our evening rubber . . .'

Dickens leaves the most graphic account of the voyage to his description of the storm the ship encountered on the third day out:

> It is the third morning. I am awakened out of my sleep by a dismal shriek from my wife, who demands to know whether there's any danger. I rouse myself, and look out of bed. The water-jug is plunging and leaping like a lively dolphin; all the smaller articles are afloat except my shoes, which are stranded on a carpet-bag, high and dry, like a couple of coal-barges. Suddenly I see them spring into the air, and behold the looking-glass, which is nailed to the wall, sticking fast upon the ceiling. At the same time the door entirely disappears, and a new one is opened in the floor. Then I begin to comprehend that the state-room is standing on its head.
>
> Before it is possible to make any arrangement at all compatible with this novel state of things, the ship rights. Before one can say, 'Thank Heaven!' she wrongs again. Before one can cry she is wrong, she seems to have started forward, and to be a creature actively running of its own accord, with broken knees and failing legs, through every variety of hole and pitfall, and stumbling constantly. Before one can so much as wonder, she takes a high leap into the air. Before she has well done that, she takes a deep dive into the water. Before she has gained the surface, she throws a summerset. The instant she is on her legs, she rushes backward. And so she goes on, staggering, heaving, wrestling, leaping, diving, jumping, pitching, throbbing, rolling, and rocking: and going through all these movements, sometimes by turns, and sometimes all together: until one feels disposed to roar for mercy.
>
> A steward passes. 'Steward!' 'Sir?' 'What *is* the matter? What *do* you call this?' 'Rather a heavy sea on, sir, and a head-wind.'
>
> A head-wind! Imagine a human face upon the vessel's prow, with fifteen thousand Sampsons in one bent upon driving her back, and hitting her exactly between the eyes whenever she attempts to advance an inch. Imagine the wind howling, the sea roaring, the rain beating: all in furious array against her. Picture the sky both dark and wild, and the clouds, in fearful sympathy with the waves, making another ocean in the air. Add to all this, the clattering on deck and down below: the tread of hurried feet; the loud hoarse shouts of seamen; the gurgling in and out of water through the scuppers; with every now and then, the striking of a heavy sea upon the planks above, – and there is the head-wind of that January morning.

However, it wasn't all that austere for some of *Britannia*'s passengers. The wines and spirits bar opened at 6 a.m., and a popular breakfast was steak with a bottle of hock. If it wasn't to the liking of Charles Dickens, who   *17* sailed back to England with another line, the *Britannia*, and all Cunard ships to follow, won the approval of the majority of sea travellers of the day by setting a remarkable standard for safety and reliability which has lasted through the years.

Charles Dickens and his fellow passengers from England, who included the Earl of Mulgrave, decided to forget their ordeal and discomfort aboard *Britannia*, and generously place on record their admiration for the way Cunard's Captain John Hewitt had brought them safely through the Atlantic storms. Captain Hewitt was presented with a set of silver plate including a unique Grecian pitcher, goblets and salver, duly inscribed:

> Presented to Captain John Hewitt of the *Britannia* Steamship, by the passengers aboard that vessel in a voyage from Liverpool to Boston, in the month of January 1842, as a slight acknowledgment of his great ability and skill, under circumstances of much difficulty and danger, and as a public token of their lasting gratitude.

The presentation was made by Charles Dickens himself after a speech by the Earl of Mulgrave who told Captain Hewitt: 'You are a sailor, Captain Hewitt, in the truest sense of the word. In all time to come, and in all your voyages upon the sea, I hope you will have a thought for those who wish to live in your memory by the help of these trifles, as they will often connect you with the pleasure of those homes and firesides from which they once wandered, and which, but for you, they might never have regained . . .'

The silver service presented to Captain Hewitt is today on display in the National Maritime Museum, Greenwich.

The most important V.I.P. on *Britannia*'s maiden voyage was the man mainly responsible for setting the standards of the new shipping line, the British and North American Royal Mail Steam Packet Company, later to become the Cunard Steam-Ship Company. He was Samuel Cunard, the line's founder, who, at the age of 51, was witnessing a life's dream coming true; a boyhood ambition of becoming the owner of the finest fleet of ships ever to sail the seas. Brought up in the seaport town of Halifax with the Atlantic Ocean on his doorstep, and with a father who started his life in the province of Nova Scotia as a dockyard carpenter, Sam Cunard had grown up one of a family of nine, with the sea, hemp and tar deep in his veins. As a boy, Sam haunted the busy Halifax waterfront with its splendid anchorage crowded with ships of many countries. It was here in 1749, 38 years before he was born, that the first 2,500 settlers landed from Britain.

Ships soon became Sam's great love, the tough men who manned them his companions; there could not have been a better place than Halifax for a young inquiring mind to learn everything there was to know about ships and shipping. Down the hill from his home he would daily watch the arrivals and departures of fishing boats and schooners, square-rigged merchantmen, privateers, whalers, frigates and cruisers of the Royal Navy. Once a month the sailing ship mail packet from Falmouth docked at the King's Wharf to be greeted by the whole town at the quayside.

Samuel Cunard, brought up with the Atlantic on his doorstep. As a boy he dreamed of owning a fleet of ships.

Sam's father, Abraham, who came from a family of respected Philadelphia shipping merchants before being banished to the British colonies following the American revolution, was a thrifty man and had soon saved enough money to buy a sailing ship to carry mails between Halifax, Newfoundland, Boston and Bermuda. It was not long before Abraham was running his own shipping company and, at the age of seventeen, Sam joined his father in the business. In 1819, Abraham Cunard retired. Sam took over with two brothers, and the business was re-named Samuel Cunard and Company.

At the age of 28, Samuel married Susan Duffus, the pretty daughter of one of Halifax's most influential merchants, and they began to raise a family. But in 1827, ten days after the birth of Susan's ninth baby, she died and Samuel was left to bring up his motherless children with the help of Grandmother Duffus.

*   *   *

To get over the tragic loss of his wife after only twelve years of marriage, Samuel Cunard worked even harder in the pursuit of his dream, and by the time he had reached fifty years of age he had become one of the richest shipping merchants of Halifax, owning and operating some forty sailing ships under the Samuel Cunard flag.

Cunard's company acquired the agency in Halifax for the Honourable East India Company, and later the General Mining Association of London. Samuel himself was appointed the first Commissioner for Lighthouses in Nova Scotia, made a director of one of the leading Nova Scotia banks, and elected to the Council of Twelve, the virtual rulers of the province. Samuel and two of his brothers also became leading stockholders in a pioneering Halifax–Quebec steamer service inaugurated by the *Royal William*, which, propelled by two 80-horsepower engines, made the first run to Quebec in six days in 1831. At that time the only other steamship in the whole of the province was a 3-horsepower ferry.

In the early 1830s Samuel Cunard took a trip to England and during his stay he was a passenger between Liverpool and Manchester on George Stephenson's 'Rocket' railway which obtained speeds of up to 47 m.p.h. This so impressed Cunard that when he returned to Halifax he informed his brothers that he was now confident that steamships, properly built and manned, would soon be able to start and arrive at ports with the punctuality of railway trains on land. The great steam revolution had dawned and a boyhood vision was about to become reality.

However, not everyone agreed with Samuel Cunard, and when he took his ideas to Boston to try and interest shipowners and merchants in a proposed Atlantic steamship fleet, he was bluntly told that the Atlantic steamship would never be anything more than a dangerous novelty and would never replace sail for trans-ocean shipping purposes. Sadly, he returned empty-handed to his home in Halifax.

Then, on November 8th, 1838, an advertisement appeared in the London *Times*: 'Steam vessels required for conveying Her Majesty's mails and Dispatches between England and Halifax, Nova Scotia, and also between England, Halifax, and New York.' Tenders were to be submitted to the Admiralty before December 15th.

Despite the fact that the copy of *The Times* containing the advertisement did not reach Samuel Cunard in Halifax until after the time limit had expired, he set sail immediately for England in a Falmouth-bound packet to submit proposals personally to the Admiralty. After weeks of negotiations, finding partners for the venture, and pulling strings behind the scenes, Cunard was awarded the contract.

As *Britannia* sailed from Liverpool on her maiden voyage the following year even a visionary like Samuel Cunard could not have foreseen that within a century, ships of the company he founded would have taken the form of giant, floating, luxury hotels, crossing the Atlantic in less than five days; even less so that the company would become involved in trans-Atlantic supersonic air travel.

CHAPTER TWO

The Battle for the Atlantic Mail Service

Less than twelve weeks passed from the day Samuel Cunard stepped off the packet at Falmouth harbour on a cold and bleak day in February 1839 to the time he signed the contract in London for the Atlantic Mail Steamer Service. The tender he had submitted to the Admiralty was for a fortnightly service between Liverpool and Halifax of wooden paddle-steamers with two feeder services, one to Boston, and the other from Pictou to Quebec when the St Lawrence was unobstructed by ice.

For this, Cunard was asking for a government subsidy of £55,000 annually, payable quarterly in advance, and for a period of ten years. The contract eventually signed on May 4th, 1839, was even better than this: Cunard was to be subsidized to the tune of £60,000 per annum for seven years, subject to twelve months' notice on either side, and with penalty clauses which included a £15,000 fine if a sailing failed to take place, and £500 per day where sailings were delayed by over twelve hours. There was a further stipulation that Cunard ships should carry a Royal Navy officer who would be responsible for the mails and, when occasion warranted, would also be responsible for the ship, superseding the captain. This latter regulation enforced by the Admiralty became the cause of friction between the appointed naval 'captains' and the company's own officers, and at a later stage Cunard was able to rid itself of the naval men on payment of a considerable sum to the government.

During the three-month period between submitting the tender and winning the contract, Samuel Cunard never worked harder, knowing well that he had come into the battle when the winner would have the chance of proving to the world that the steamship was on its way to replacing sail, and had come to stay. He also knew it was a time that would be memorable for far-reaching postal reforms in Britain. The Admiralty contract was to enable a cheaper steamship packet rate to be fixed at one shilling and twopence per letter carried across the Atlantic.*

Being a colonist from a Philadelphian family of Quakers with Teutonic backgrounds did not help Cunard when he found himself up against two rival British shipping companies which had already submitted tenders –

---

*One shilling and twopence sterling equalled one shilling and fourpence in Canada and, shortly before Cunard was awarded the new mail service, a Canadian deputation came to London to protest to the British Government over the high cost of trans-Atlantic mail, bringing with them proof that some letters were costing over five shillings and taking sixty-five days.

the St George Steam Packet Company, owners of *Sirius*, which in April 1838 had won the prize for being the first steamer to cross the Atlantic from England to America; and the Great Western Steamship Company, owners of the *Great Western*, already the doyen of the early steamers. Cunard had one trick up his sleeve, however, which he appears to have used to maximum effect – the advantage of having friends who had friends in high places. One of them was the Hon. Mrs Caroline Norton, a well known London society beauty, a grand-daughter of the dramatist Richard Sheridan, and herself a novelist and poetess of note.

Cunard had made a large circle of friends in London during the years preceding his trip to tender for the Atlantic mails. It had almost become a habit of his to spend part of each winter in England bringing over from Halifax some of his older children, and his brother and partner, Joe Cunard. In London he kept a suite of rooms at a Piccadilly hotel, and a small office in the city.

Mrs Norton included among her friends members of the peerage, politicians, and the literary set including the Irish poet, Thomas Moore, and Benjamin Disraeli, then better known for his writing than as a parliamentarian. Through Mrs Norton, Cunard established amicable relations with a number of members of the government.

It was around this time that Mrs Norton's husband, the Hon. George Norton, scandalized England by publicly accusing his wife of having an affair with Lord Melbourne, the Prime Minister who became Queen Victoria's confidential adviser in the early days of her reign. The Norton scandal came to nothing and was finally laid to rest as part of a political smear campaign by Lord Melbourne's enemies; Mrs Norton's character remained untarnished; and Samuel Cunard was able to continue looking upon Mrs Norton as a useful friend to further his cause. Just how useful Mrs Norton may have been was hinted at by Fanny Kemble, the actress and writer daughter of Sarah Siddons.

Fanny Kemble, whose role as Juliet filled Covent Garden for three years, wrote in an autobiography, *Record of a Girlhood*, that Mrs Norton often came to parties at her home: 'On one occasion I remember her asking us to dine at her uncle's,' she wrote. 'Among the people we met were Lord Lansdowne and Lord Normanby, both then in the Ministry, and whose goodwill and influence she was then exerting herself to captivate on behalf of a certain, shy, rather rustic gentleman, from the far away province of New Brunswick, Mr Samuel Cunard.'

Whether or not Caroline Norton's influence on their lordships from the Ministry, or on the ears of the Prime Minister and Queen's adviser had any effect in Samuel Cunard being eventually awarded the mail contract is pure conjecture. In any case, there was little doubt that Cunard had offered the Admiralty the best of the deals, and had convinced Sir Edward Parry, the newly appointed Comptroller of Steam Machinery and Packet Service at the Admiralty, that the ships he was planning to build would provide the best regular and reliable service across the Atlantic. And so it proved.

James Melville, the secretary of the East India Company, was a friend of Cunard's, and he advised him to try and persuade Robert Napier, the famous Clyde shipbuilder and engineer, to build the first Atlantic mail steamers. Robert Napier's firm, Wood and Napier, had obtained a position of pre-eminence in Scottish shipbuilding by the end of the 1830s, Wood being responsible for first-class hulls, and Napier for the development of greatly improved side-lever engines. For ten years the firm had been building coastal and Isle of Man packets including the successful steamship *Bernice* for the East India Company, and *Queen of the Isles*, another steamship which was to serve as a model for the first Atlantic Cunarder, *Britannia*.

Cunard made his initial approach to Napier on February 25th, 1839, telling him bluntly that he required plain and comfortable ships with the least unnecessary expense for show. He knew that dependability and safety, not luxury for passengers, were going to be the keys to success if he was to keep going a fortnightly service throughout the year against all the hazards and unpredictability of Atlantic weather. He also wanted to prove to those who had laughed at his dreams of a regular trans-Atlantic steamship service how wrong they had been.

A month after approaching Napier the first contract to build the ships was drawn up. This was for the construction of three wooden paddle-wheel steamships each not less than 200 feet long, not less than 32 feet beam, and not less than 21 feet 6 inches depth of hold from top of timbers to underside of deck amidships. The cabins were to be appointed in a neat and comfortable manner for the accommodation of from 60 to 70 passengers. Each vessel was to be fitted by Napier with two steam engines, having cylinders 70 inches in diameter and with 6-feet, 6-inch stroke.

These specifications were being continually altered in consequence of further talks between Samuel Cunard and the Admiralty, and when the final agreement to build was ratified, a fourth ship was added to the order, and the tonnage of each ship went up to 1,154 tons.

Knowing the engine was to be the key to a regular and strictly time-keeping service across the Atlantic, Robert Napier, who had some revolutionary ideas on how a steamer should be operated, passed on some tips to Cunard, all of which were acted upon. These included the placing of a first-class engineer in charge of the engine room, with trained personnel under him; and building into the ships complete workshops, with tools and replacement parts in case of breakdowns. Up to the middle of the 19th century shipowners had run steamships like sailing ships, not appreciating that a different kind of crew was required for steam.

Then came Samuel Cunard's search for capital and partners to join him. Again he was lucky, this time through Robert Napier, who introduced him to two hard-headed Scottish shipowners, George Burns and David Mac-Iver. Both were immediately attracted by the possibility of founding a regular trans-Atlantic service of steamships, particularly when they heard that Cunard had the Admiralty mail contract 'in his pocket'.

As a result of Cunard-Burns-MacIver talks, George Burns and David

George Burns, a hard-headed Scottish ship-owner, who helped Samuel Cunard form his first mail packet company with a capital of £270,000.

MacIver paid £25,000 for a half interest in the mail contract plus a half share of the mail vessels. A company was formed and £270,000 capital was raised, Samuel Cunard putting in £55,000 for his shares. The company was called The British and North American Royal Mail Steam Packet Company but it was such a long name that it was soon being called 'Cunard's Company' by the general public, later to become officially the Cunard Steam-Ship Company, the name that remains to this day.

At the outset, George Burns was left in Glasgow to supervise construction of the company's ships on the Clyde; David MacIver went to Liverpool to organize the Liverpool terminus; and Samuel Cunard sailed for New York with one of his sons to establish the Boston and Halifax branches of the company.

Britannia was built by R. Duncan and Co., Greenock, and launched in February 1840. Her three sister ships, *Acadia*, *Caledonia* and *Columbia*, all built on the Clyde, followed in the same year.

The arrival of *Britannia* on her first trans-Atlantic trip at both Halifax and Boston was described in great detail on the front pages of American and Nova Scotia newspapers. The *Halifax Recorder* of July 18th, 1840, said:

At a very early hour yesterday morning the elegant new steamship *Britannia* came up the harbour. She left Liverpool on the 4th inst., at half-past two p.m., thus making the passage, in spite of head winds the whole time, in 12 days and 12 hours. She had brought 63 passengers, and among the number we are happy to congratulate His Lordship, the Bishop of Nova Scotia and family, and the Hon. S. Cunard, on their return to 'Sweet Home'.

Caledonia, one of *Britannia's* three sister ships.

A pilot was taken on board off Scateri on Thursday, and although her arrival was generally looked for since Monday last, her appearance excited surprise as much as if she had come unexpectedly.

She is built long and narrow, and there seems to be a felicitous combination of grandeur, elegance, speed and durability in her construction and material. She is propelled by two sets of paddles, and her spars and rigging very much enhance her beauty.

The report went on to describe the main news in newspapers brought by *Britannia* from England which told of an attempt on the life of Queen Victoria and Prince Albert by a man named Edward Oxford who 'fired two pistol shots on June 10th at Her Majesty while out for an airing. Oxford was presumed to be insane. No one was injured.'

The report continued:

Britannia went from here to Boston where great preparations were made to give her a hearty Yankee welcome, but the lateness of the hour, ten o'clock Saturday night, of her arrival there prevented the manifestation of feeling which would otherwise have been the case.

Nevertheless, she was saluted by the Revenue Cutter *Hamilton* which was brilliantly illuminated, and salutes were also fired from Long Wharf, from East Boston and from South Boston, and the band aboard *Columbus* played 'God Save the Queen'. Notwithstanding her late arrival she was heartily greeted by many citizens assembled on the wharves.

Three days later, on July 21st, Boston proclaimed the day 'Cunard Festival Day' and a parade of citizens, headed by government and civic leaders of all the New England States, marched eight abreast through the streets. The day ended with a great banquet given in honour of Samuel Cunard and attended by 2,300 people. The banquet was held in a spacious and elegantly decorated pavilion with 'plazzas' converted into galleries, and ornamented with flags. In the centre of the 'plazzas' an arch rose bearing the inscription: 'LIVERPOOL–HALIFAX–BOSTON' with the name 'CUNARD' at the base.

The main toast by the dinner's president was: 'Health, happiness, and prosperity to Mr Cunard and may he meet with the success, and enjoy the honours, which are his due in both of the countries he has now united.'

For several days Samuel Cunard and *Britannia* were front-page news in the New England newspapers. One journalist wrote: 'Never since the arrival of the Pilgrim Fathers have the shores of America experienced so important an event.' Another went even further and declared in his newspaper: 'Since the discovery of America by Columbus, nothing has occurred of so much importance to the new world as navigating the Atlantic by steamers.' Whether or not the newspapers of the day exaggerated the importance of the occasion, there was no doubt about the effect the new steamship service had on Boston itself. Business began to flourish, 25 trade with Canada and Europe greatly increased, and Boston recovered much of the importance that she had enjoyed at the beginning of the century.

It was all put down to the Cunard steamship packets, which not only set a standard for regularity and dependability, but, with every docking, brought more and more trade, together with regular mail and news. The steamers also helped to increase the population of Boston from 85,000 in 1840, to 114,000 in 1845. The only sour note was that all this caused a great deal of friction between New York and Boston because the people of New York considered Cunard should have made their city and port the terminal for the new mail steamers.

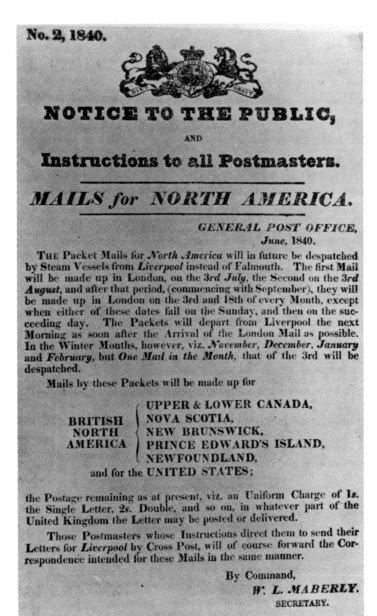

No. 2, 1840.

NOTICE TO THE PUBLIC,

AND

Instructions to all Postmasters.

MAILS *for* NORTH AMERICA.

GENERAL POST OFFICE,
June, 1840.

THE Packet Mails for *North America* will in future be despatched by Steam Vessels from *Liverpool* instead of Falmouth. The first Mail will be made up in London, on the 3rd *July,* the Second on the *3rd August,* and after that period, (commencing with September), they will be made up in London on the 3rd and 18th of every Month, except when either of these dates fall on the Sunday, and then on the succeeding day. The Packets will depart from Liverpool the next Morning as soon after the Arrival of the London Mail as possible. In the Winter Months, however, viz. *November, December, January* and *February,* but *One Mail in the Month,* that of the 3rd will be despatched.

Mails by these Packets will be made up for

	UPPER & LOWER CANADA,
BRITISH	NOVA SCOTIA,
NORTH	NEW BRUNSWICK,
AMERICA	PRINCE EDWARD'S ISLAND,
	NEWFOUNDLAND,

and for the UNITED STATES;

the Postage remaining as at present, viz. an Uniform Charge of **1*s.*** the Single Letter, 2*s.* Double, and so on, in whatever part of the United Kingdom the Letter may be posted or delivered.

Those Postmasters whose Instructions direct them to send their Letters for *Liverpool* by Cross Post, will of course forward the Correspondence intended for these Mails in the same manner.

By Command,

W. L. MABERLY.

SECRETARY.

A General Post Office notice of 1840 announcing the inauguration of the Cunard transatlantic mail service. Single letters from England to America cost one shilling.

CHAPTER THREE

The Atlantic Takes its Toll

The dependability of the Cunard service across the dangerous waters of the Atlantic proved a success, and within a few years of *Britannia*'s maiden voyage, Samuel Cunard had won from the Admiralty a three-fold increase in the subsidy to his line. It was a hard-earned reward, for in the growing Atlantic shipping trade the sea was taking a heavy toll of ships, both sail and steam, and some shipping lines were ruined by the loss of a single vessel.

Less than a year after *Britannia*'s launch, *President*, the wonder ship of the British and American Steam Navigation Company of London, sailing from New York to Liverpool with 136 passengers, vanished without trace in mid-Atlantic. When launched in 1840, *President*, with 2,366 tons, was acclaimed the largest ship in the world, surpassing everything yet known in luxury and comfort. Her loss was not only looked upon as a major catastrophe, it helped swell the ranks of a growing anti-steam faction on both sides of the Atlantic – people who asserted that steam was a passing novelty which would never take the place of sail. The loss of *President* put her owners out of business.

And in the summer of 1843, when Cunard had been operating across the Atlantic exactly three years, one of the first of the four in the mail fleet, *Columbia*, went aground in the fog on a rock near Seal Island, just outside Halifax. Luckily no lives were lost and all the mail and cargo was saved.

The occasion, nevertheless, was a dramatic one. Samuel Cunard was in Halifax at the time awaiting *Columbia*'s arrival from Boston with eighty-five passengers. When she was nearly two days overdue and the whole town was out, anxious to sight her, *Acadia*, the sister ship to *Columbia*, came into port with the news that *Columbia* had been carried off course and was firmly stuck on a reef called the Devil's Limb. *Columbia*'s plight had been discovered when three schooners out of Boston, steering the same route, had also been carried off course by strong currents and heard *Columbia*'s distress guns.

In a remarkable rescue operation, all passengers, with the help of a lightkeeper and *Columbia*'s crew, were able to scramble ashore onto an island where, together with the salvaged mail, they were picked up by Samuel Cunard who had sailed to the rescue in one of his Halifax steamers. *Columbia* was a complete loss, but three schooner-loads of her cargo and equipment were taken off before she broke up with the coming of the first storms. The rescued passengers and mail sailed on another Cunard ship from Halifax and were only a week late on arrival in England.

A new Cunard paddle-steamer, *Hibernia*, her tonnage increased to 1,422 tons, was soon to replace *Columbia*, and four years later she inaugurated the long hoped for Cunard Liverpool–New York service – a service to become world-famous and maintained by Cunard until 1969.

Hibernia inaugurated the first Liverpool to New York service in 1857 – a service to become famous through two centuries.

It was not only storms, rocks and icebergs that took the toll of Atlantic shipping in the nineteenth century. The fear of a steamship catching fire, with thousands of tons of coal aboard for the hungry furnaces, was a constant dread. In 1848, *Ocean Monarch*, a fine ship owned by Enoch Train's White Diamond Line, which had just beaten the Cunarder *Britannia* by a few hours on a voyage to New York, caught fire on one of her next Atlantic trips shortly after leaving Liverpool. Four hundred passengers and crew lost their lives and it was one of the greatest sea catastrophes of the time.

A study of available records of the trans-Atlantic packets of the mid-nineteenth century reads today like a memorial '. . . wrecked near Liverpool, 1839; . . . wrecked New York Bar, 1843; . . . burned out East River Pier, 1849; . . . burned in Mersey off Liverpool, 1855; . . . went missing London–New York . . . foundered at sea, 1855; . . . wrecked near Cherbourg; . . . wrecked Goodwin Sands; . . . sunk after collision in Irish channel; . . . posted missing with 600 aboard'.

Even *Britannia* nearly came to a sad end in February 1844, trapped by ice in Boston Harbour. It was the first time in living memory that Boston Harbour had frozen over and *Britannia* was gripped in ice several feet thick. When her wooden hull was in danger of being crushed the people of Boston decided to show their affection and indebtedness to the Cunard ship and service by cutting her out of the ice. The merchants of the city got together and raised enough money to employ gangs of lumberjacks and

28

labourers to cut a winding, seven-mile long channel through the ice from the Cunard docks to the edge of the ice-free sea. In a remarkable operation, hundreds of men and horses worked day and night cutting up the ice in great blocks and hauling them away. Two days later *Britannia* was escorted down the newly cut channel to freedom by cheering Bostonians, many keeping up alongside her on skates and sleighs.

The original agreement drawn up by the committee of Boston merchants for freeing *Britannia* from the ice is today on display as a maritime exhibit at the Old State House, Boston, Massachusetts, and states:

> Mr John Hill in connexion with Messrs. Gage Hittinger and Co., agree to cut out a passage for the Steamship *Britannia* to proceed to sea tomorrow night and to cut the passage from the Eastern Ferry way as far as India Wharf, the whole passage way to be 200-feet wide at least; the whole to be accomplished within three days from the first day of February at sunrise and they agree to receive in full for their services the sum of fifteen hundred dollars to be paid when the work is accomplished and to receive no pay if they do not accomplish it as stipulated. Boston, 31 Jan. 1844.

When Cunard asked for the fifteen hundred dollar bill they were told there was nothing to pay. The merchants, grateful to the trade *Britannia* had brought to their port, had settled that.

The part Cunard played in helping to keep the public's faith in the dependability of their ships was to a great extent due to their captains, and there was no better example than Captain C.H.E. Judkin, one of the first of the company's commanders. Born in Chester, England, his first command was the *Britannia*, which he joined in the autumn of 1840. At the end of his first outward voyage from Liverpool, which commenced on October 20th of that year, the passengers addressed him an appreciative letter which ran as follows:

> R.M.S. *Britannia*
> November 2nd, 1840
>
> Sir,
>   We cannot leave the *Britannia* without expressing to you the very sincere satisfaction we have experienced during our passage from Liverpool, and we feel much pleasure in marking our sense of the diligent and attentive consideration you have throughout devoted to the comfort of the passengers as well as to the other interests of the vessel committed to your charge.

Captain C.H.E. Judkin, one of Cunard's first commanders. During his career with the company he commanded all Cunard ships except one, and faced many dangerous and hazardous Atlantic crossings, always getting his ship home.

Captain Judkin's exceptional navigational abilities were highly appreciated by all, while the crew who served under him vied with each other in rendering good and faithful service, according to records kept at the time. With passengers too he was exceedingly popular for they 29

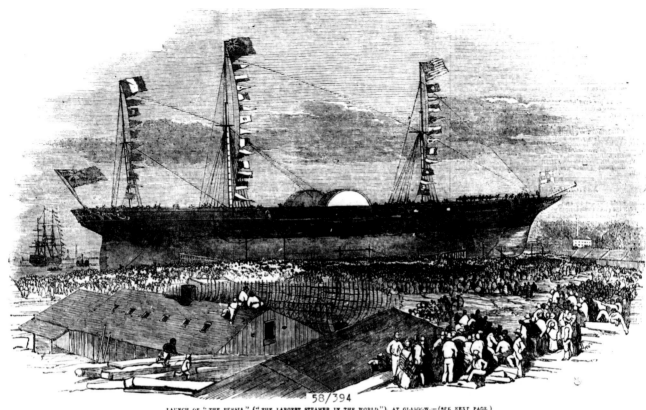

LAUNCH OF " THE PERSIA " (" THE LARGEST STEAMER IN THE WORLD "), AT GLASGOW.—(SEE NEXT PAGE.)

admired both his personality and the care he devoted to ensuring their safety and comfort.

Persia, described as 'the largest steamer in the world' at its launch in 1856.

During his career with Cunard (he retired in 1871) he was captain of all ships except one, and faced many dangerous and hazardous crossings of the Atlantic, always getting his ship home. On the *Cambria* in March 1852, the ship arrived at Halifax two days late and in a crippled condition after being held up in an icefield which necessitated a long detour to the south in tempestuous weather during which both the ship's paddles were badly smashed. Newspaper reports recorded that the *Cambria*'s safe arrival on the other side of the Atlantic was due mainly to the captain, 'which spoke volumes in praise of the noble line to which the ship belongs, and the exemplary conduct and skill displayed by her Commander and officers'.

Prior to the first sailing of *Persia* on January 26th, 1856, at a luncheon on board attended by shipping and civic officials of Liverpool, the hope was expressed that the *Persia* would overtake her rival, the U.S. owned *Pacific*, which already had a three-day start. Captain Judkin replied that he would endeavour to do his duty, as in the past, and ever have regard for safety before speed. The *Persia* arrived safely in New York; the *Pacific* failed to arrive and was posted missing.

30   The success of the first Cunard Atlantic mail fleet was due to other factors

apart from the dependability of the ships and the general high standard of efficiency aboard. Ashore, the brilliant partnership of Samuel Cunard, George Burns and David MacIver helped to hand-pick the crews, find the passengers and cargoes, keep the ships to schedule, and administer the business always with an eye to future expansion and eventual supremacy over the North Atlantic. The three men had distinctive qualities: Cunard, a diplomat with the foresight of a genius, brought energy and personal charm to the partnership; George Burns, already a wealthy shipping merchant by the time he joined Cunard, contributed shrewdness and expertise in all shipbuilding matters; and David MacIver, of first-rate executive ability, was the one with the knowledge of men, and the experience of discipline to keep morale and efficiency at the highest level. Sadly, David MacIver did not live long enough to fully enjoy the success of the company he helped to found, and died in 1845.

The Cunard company had also built up a reputation for safety which went far to gain the confidence of passengers, a fact which later determined its success against all attempts to decry the new form of propulsion by the owners of sailing packet fleets, particularly the Americans. In 1841 many Americans refused to see steamships supplanting the sailing packets and the *New York Herald* stated: 'There is to be somewhat of a contest this year between our far-famed sailing packets and the steamships. It is yet to be discovered which are the most comfortable and profitable.'

It was therefore not unexpected that Cunard's main competitors first came from America where the people were finding it extremely galling to take second place to a British concern although it was mainly their own fault in being slow in changing to steam.

The opening of Cunard's New York service in 1847 marked the turning point in the conquest of steam over sail and from then on the grand old American sailing packets, with their luxury appointed cabins, began to disappear, and the Cunard fleet, with the building of four more steamers, *America*, *Niagara*, *Europe* and *Canada*, began to rule the Atlantic waves. These four new vessels carried navigation lights, well ahead of the then general practice, and Cunard had renegotiated their contract to give weekly services to New York for eight months of the year, and fortnightly services in the winter.

It wasn't long before the American public demanded something should be done to compete with the growth and success of the Cunard Line. The answer came in the form of a new shipping line, the New York and Liverpool United States Mail Steamship Company, soon to become known as the Collins Line, which was generously subsidized by the United States Government with a sum nearly double that paid by the British Government to Cunard. One of the conditions of the U.S. Government contract with Collins was that the company's ships should be capable of 'outstripping' the Cunarders.

The man behind the new American line was Edward Knight Collins, a New Englander and a prominent New York packet operator who came from a long line of sea captains.

CUNARD LINE
STEAM TO NEW YORK

THE FULL-POWERED SCREW STEAMER
SIDON,
TO SAIL
19TH MAY.
SIX GUINEAS
FULL DIETARY.

Apply to JAMES BAINES & CO., Tower Buildnigs, Water
Street, Liverpool; or to
W. D. MATHEWS & CO,
Merchants & Ship Agents, PENZANCE, Sole Agents.

On April 27th, 1850, the first of the Collins Line 'side-wheeler' (the
American term for 'paddle') steamships, *Atlantic*, sailed from Liverpool,
soon to be followed by her sister ships, *Arctic*, *Pacific* and *Baltic*. In both
speed and comfort the new Collins Line ships surpassed all Cunard ships,
each one being approximately 1,000 tons larger than the average Cunarder. Soon, Collins were carrying more passengers between Liverpool and
New York than Cunard. Up to 1850, Cunard ships had been making the

Atlantic crossing eastwards in eleven to twelve days, and westward in twelve to thirteen. The Collins Line steamers began crossing in under ten days, setting up new records. Passenger accommodation was far superior on the Collins Line. Bathrooms and barber shops were provided and all ships were fitted with a new electric bell system to state rooms. The steam-heated public rooms had thick, flowered carpets, crimson velvet sofas, brocade hangings and seashell-shaped spittoons.

Both the government and the Post Office in London began to get a little anxious about the situation and in 1853 a commission was appointed to enquire into the Mail Packet Contracts. Samuel Cunard wasted no time in putting his case for the Atlantic contract to be continued in his favour, and in a letter written from the Burlington Hotel, London, on March 11th, 1853, to Viscount Canning, the then postmaster-general and under-secretary for state, he wrote:

> It may not be considered improper on my part to bring before the Commission the circumstances under which my Contract was originally commenced.
> The Mails for America were formerly carried by the old Ten Gun Brigs, at a cost of £40,000 a year, these Vessels were unsuited for the purpose, and the Service was very irregularly performed, the passage occupying from thirty to seventy days. Many of the ships were lost with all the passengers and crew – indeed, they were designated 'Coffins'.
> I had made many passages in the old Brigs and was well aware of the danger and uncertainty attached to them, and I had lost many friends by them, which induced me to turn my attention to the subject . . .
> When the American Line (Collins) came on with the aid of their Government, they did not hesitate to declare they would run every British Steamer off the Atlantic and it was very obvious to me that we must either resign the supremacy to them, confining ourselves to our 400 Horse Power Boats which were safe and good Vessels, or take effective and immediate measures to meet our powerful opponents. I adopted the latter course.

Cunard then went on to explain how he and his partners were building more powerful ships to keep ambitious competitors in check, adding:

> If the Government can preserve this Line of beautiful Steamers, sustaining itself by the postage, or even if it should cost something in addition, the Country will be benefited by it, in having a safe weekly communication for the Government Dispatches and Mails.

The letter concluded:

> These are circumstances which together with the manner in which

the Service has been performed for thirteen years, that will, I trust, entitle me to the consideration of the Government and to the continuance of this Contract while I may wish to retain it.

I have the honour to be,
With great respect,
Your obedient Servant,   *S. Cunard*

Edward Collins was soon threatening to 'sweep all Cunarders off the Atlantic'. His threats could not have been better timed, for between the years 1854 and 1856 Britain was at war with Russia and Cunard's contract specified that not only were all Cunard mail ships to be built stoutly enough to carry large calibre guns, but they could also be requisitioned as troop carriers in the event of war. When Britain went to war in the Crimea, all British mail services across the Atlantic – except the service to Boston – ceased, and eleven of Cunard's Atlantic steamers were taken over to be operated under Admiralty orders.

Arabia, built in Greenock in 1852, carried the horses of the Light Brigade to Balaclava, 200 at a time suspended in canvas slings. Other Cunard ships transported troops to battle, and the wounded from Balaclava, across the Black Sea to the hospital at Scutari where Florence Nightingale was working with her volunteer band of 38 nurses shipped out from England. Among other Cunard ships which saw active service during the Crimean War were the three paddle-steamers, *Niagara*, *Cambria* and *Europa*, and two of the first Cunarders to be iron built and propeller driven, *Andes* and *Alps*.

Little has been written about the role of the British merchant ships in the Crimean War, but the log of Captain John Muir of the *Andes* (1,275 tons, built in 1852 by Denny Bros, Dumbarton, Scotland) gives some idea of what both vessels and men had to endure.

The log opens on Sunday, April 16th, 1854, when the *Andes* left

Liverpool for Devonport to embark troops and continues until November 16th when, with 1,100 French troops on board, she was anchored in Constantinople harbour awaiting further orders. During those long seven months, *Andes* spent much of her time helping evacuate sick and wounded British soldiers and the log tells of crowded quarters, the great heat and outbreaks of cholera which made conditions so bad that hardly a day passed without a death aboard, with the ship having to be constantly fumigated with gunpowder and sulphur.

In early November the *Andes* was sent along the coast to Georgia to pick up Turkish troops for Balaclava. Anchored in Balaclava Bay on November 5th, Captain Muir recorded: 'There was a fearful engagement between our troops and the Russians. They surprised our troops in the grey of the morning. We lost about 3,000 killed and wounded; the Russians lost about 10, or 12,000. Battle lasted from 6 a.m. till 3.30 p.m. in the defeat of the Russians.'

Many of the British wounded in the Battle of Balaclava were put aboard the *Andes* which returned to Scutari and went on to Constantinople where, on November 6th, the log ends.

England and France committed 405,000 men to the Crimea, of whom 25,600 were killed in action; another 38,800 died of disease, mostly cholera.

At the end of the Crimean War, Cunard answered the Collins threat by producing two new ships designed for speed, *Asia* and *Africa*, and the battle was on again, with *Asia* recapturing the record for the eastern

The after deck aboard one of Cunard's first mail ships, *Asia*, built in 1850. At the end of the Crimean War she recaptured the record for the Atlantic eastern crossing.

35

crossing by bringing it down to ten days, seven hours; but *Asia* was soon to be outstripped by new Collins ships, and *Africa*, one of the last wooden Cunarders, fared no better against her American rivals.

The fickle British public looked upon the latest ascendancy of the American ships as a loss of prestige for Britain, and *Punch*, the London magazine of humour and political satire founded in 1841, mirrored their thoughts with the following contribution:

> *A steamer of the Collins Line,*
> *A Yankee Doodle Notion,*
> *Has also quickest cut the brine*
> *Across the Atlantic Ocean,*
> *And British agents, no way slow*
> *Her merits to discover,*
> *Have been and bought her — just to tow*
> *The Cunard packets over.*

Because of the immediate success of the American steamers and their superiority over Cunard, the Admiralty and the British Post Office ordered the company to improve the size and tonnage of their Atlantic fleet. In return the mail contract was renewed for a further twelve years.

Persia was another Cunard ship built to compete against the Collins Line in 1856. The largest vessel of her time on the North Atlantic, she was 376 feet in length, with a tonnage of 3,300. Although very expensive to run because of the vast quantities of coal she consumed, *Persia* came to the rescue and set up a new record crossing time of nine days, four hours, and forty-five minutes. The outcome of the Cunard-Collins struggle came tragically and unexpectedly, and was blamed on the reckless speed of Collins ships, which were expected by their owners to beat the Cunarders, regardless of weather and hazards, whereas Cunard captains were instructed never to put speed ahead of safety.

The enforced speed of the American ships strained engines to breaking point and after most voyages costly repairs had to be made. It also meant heavy coal consumption and the line soon began to lose money while Cunard continued to show profits. In September 1854, the Collins ship *Arctic* collided with a small French steamer *Vesta* off Cape Race, and foundered, with the loss of 322 lives including the wife, son and daughter of Edward Knight Collins. Eighteen months later, *Pacific*, sailing from Liverpool with 186 passengers, and determined to beat the new Cunarder *Persia*, departing about the same time, went missing without trace and was presumed to have struck an iceberg.

In 1858 the Collins Line collapsed in financial ruin.

The Cunard Line steamed on.

CHAPTER FOUR

Sir Samuel Rules the Waves

Samuel Cunard had been against his ships being required for war duties and the clause specifying that Cunard mail packets could be requisitioned in time of war, absent from the original contract, had been introduced at a later stage. He considered the two services, the Mercantile Marine and the Royal Navy, should not be combined, but once the clause was written into his government contract he had no option but to comply strictly with its provisions, and did so to the letter. His personal feelings against having his mail packets armed and used by the Admiralty as troop carriers when needed, did not, however, stop members of the House of Commons applauding the contribution of the Cunard Line during a debate on the conduct of the Crimean War, and some M.P.s went as far as to assert that 'Mr Cunard's ships' played a great part in helping to win the war.

During the Commons debate, the Prime Minister, Lord Palmerston, a former Lord of the Admiralty, asked for the Christian name of 'this Mr Cunard', and on being told was heard to say, more to himself than to the assembled members, 'Sir Samuel Cunard — yes, it sounds well!' But Samuel Cunard had to wait another three years to have his work as the pioneer of the Atlantic steamship route and contributor to the Crimean War effort honoured. Shortly after the Commons debate, the Palmerston Government fell, and it was March 1859, when Palmerston had been returned to power, before the following announcement was made from Whitehall: 'The Queen has been pleased to direct letters patent to be passed under the Great Seal, granting the dignity of a Baronet of the United Kingdom of Great Britain and Ireland unto Samuel Cunard of Bush Hill.'

It was the greatest moment in Samuel Cunard's life and he celebrated the occasion with his children and grandchildren in fine style at his new home, Bush Hill House, Edmonton, North London, a country mansion set in 74 acres of parkland, which he was renting on a ten-year lease. For his coat of arms, Sir Samuel chose three anchors crested by a falcon on a rock, one claw resting on a cinquefoil, and the motto, 'By perseverance'. It could hardly have been more apt.

When Samuel Cunard was made a baronet he had reached the age of seventy-two and was a grandfather with thirty-six grandchildren. He was already being referred to as the undisputed king of the Atlantic, and he had reached the pinnacle of all his dreams and ambitions. There were no more peaks on his horizon to climb, no more storms to weather, and he was content to spend much of his time in his new London home with his grandchildren, and leave the worries of running a great shipping line to 37

Samuel Cunard shortly after becoming Sir Samuel Cunard, a baronet of the United Kingdom of Great Britain and Ireland.

two of his sons, Edward, the eldest, then aged 44, and William, 10 years younger.

All three original partners had made arrangements that their interests, on their death or retirement, should be carried on by those chosen from within their families, and outsiders should be kept out. So, early in the company's history, elder sons and relations were being trained to take over control, and Samuel Cunard had nominated Edward and William. On the death of the first David MacIver in 1845, his brother Charles took over.

By 1855, the capital reserves of the Cunard, Burns and MacIver families were employed in two separate companies, the original British and North American Royal Mail Steam Packet Company, trading across the Atlantic, and the British and Foreign Steam Navigation Company, operating

Charles MacIver took over from his brother, David, in 1845 and carried on the Cunard policy of safety at sea. His 'orders to captains' stated: 'The trust of so many lives under your charge is a great trust.'

between the United Kingdom and Mediterranean ports.

Delegation of work among the three families worked well during the time Samuel Cunard was alive and active. Samuel's son, Edward, took control of the Halifax, Boston and New York end of the business, and, together with his father, was responsible for eastbound cargoes and passenger bookings as well as the servicing of ships in Canadian and American ports. Father and son also represented the company in all negotiations with the American Government relating to the operation and renewal of mail contracts.

Charles MacIver took sole control in Liverpool over the servicing and management of ships, and was given wide discretion in seeing that the Cunard policy of safety at sea, discipline and efficiency was carried out. Some idea of the care which the company took to keep its captains and crews alert to the dangers of the Atlantic is given in Charles MacIver's '*Orders to Captains*' of 1848, when he wrote:

> We rely on your keeping every person attached to the ship, both officers and people throughout the several departments, up to the highest standard of discipline and efficiency which we expect in the service.
>
> The trust of so many lives under the captain's charge is a great trust. It will require great vigilance, day and night. Good steering is of great value. Pick out some of the best helmsmen for this duty. Let them steer the whole voyage out and home – such sailors to be paid five shillings per month extra wages, ranking as quartermasters. Canvas is not to be used except for steadying the vessel in a gale. The officer of the watch is expected to count the revolutions of the engine every two hours.
>
> It is also to be borne in mind that every part of the coast board of England and Ireland should be read off by the lead, and ships from abroad making their landfall should never omit to verify their positions by soundings. Masters eager to obtain the credit of making a short passage rather than lose a few minutes in heaving the ship to, will run the risk of losing the vessel and all the lives on board.

Orders were also given that everything should be done to avoid ice and icebergs during the winter and spring months.

The Burns brothers, and later the two sons of George Burns, concerned themselves mostly with ship construction on the Clyde, and negotiating successive mail contracts with the British Government.

Like most families, not all Cunard, Burns and MacIver members held the same views, and during the forty years of the three-family partnership there were occasions when behind-the-scenes differences caused concern. The most serious, which came to near disaster for Samuel Cunard, was caused by his younger brother, Joseph, who had grown up into a tough, brash, go-getter, and thought that anything Samuel could do he could do better. Unfortunately, Joseph had none of his elder brother's caution and diplomacy. Joe started his working life in charge of a timber business 39 owned by Samuel's Halifax company on the banks of the River Miramichi in Northern New Brunswick. The timber business was run from the port of Chatham at the river's mouth and, within a few years, Joe had opened four shipyards, employed most of the town of Chatham, and lived in a magnificent home like a feudal Lord.

It wasn't long before the word was going around that Joe had over-reached himself and owed money everywhere. In 1842 he was near bankruptcy, but he managed to keep his money troubles away from Sam and weather the storm for a time. In 1849 Joe Cunard's 'empire' in New Brunswick collapsed; the timber mills and shipyards closed; a brickworks and fish-packing plant shut down; and the town of Chatham was ruined, with most of the population put out of work. The townspeople turned on Joe and he only escaped an angry mob which had gathered outside his offices by arming himself with two pistols, jumping on a horse, and galloping to the coast, where he took a ship to England and was never seen in New Brunswick again.

When the news of Joe's financial collapse reached Samuel in London he took the first available ship back to Halifax to discover that his own business there, S. Cunard and Company, was also in danger of collapse because he was a partner in a number of Joe's subsidiary companies and his brother's creditors were demanding payment from him.

Samuel issued a statement guaranteeing that all his brother's debts would be met in full. It took months for Samuel to sort out the mess, and many years to pay back all the money. But his generosity didn't stop there. He even advanced Joe enough cash to set up in business again in Liverpool, where, in partnership with a friend, Joe started the firm of Cunard, Wilson and Company, ship valuers and brokers. When Joe died in 1864, leaving a wife and four children, he had once again become prosperous, was looked upon as one of Liverpool's leading citizens, and received an obituary tribute in *The Times*.

The biggest upset within the MacIver family came in the mid 1850s over the running of a Mediterranean part of the business. David, the son, believed that the type of ships being used by the Cunard company were out-dated. In one letter, David MacIver wrote: 'I have for years urged persistently that the class of vessel on which my father prides himself has "run its day" as far as the Mediterranean is concerned. I have no shadow of doubt that the present class of Cunard steamer is destined to be "elbowed out" of the Mediterranean by such steamers as I propose to build.'

David then went about obtaining the Mediterranean agency for himself, severed his connection with Cunard, and threatened to start a new company of rival steamships to the Mediterranean. For a time, father and son were hardly on speaking terms. David's plans came to nothing, however, and he started a new shipping line from Liverpool to Bombay under the title of David MacIver and Company. Later he abandoned shipping, embarked upon a political career, and became a Member of Parliament.

The most serious disagreement in the Cunard, Burns, MacIver partnership also happened in the middle of the 1850s over the big maritime question of the time – paddle-wheels or screw-propellers? This time the two partners who fell out and caused a parting of the ways were Samuel Cunard and the man who had backed him from the start of the Atlantic mail service, George Burns. When it came to arguments over policy matters, both men could be stubborn adversaries; on this occasion Burns held the view that the Cunard Atlantic ships should change to propellers, and Samuel Cunard believed there was little incentive to introduce change while the mail contract continued providing them with a good income as long as ships kept to schedule. The disagreement boiled over to become a test of strength between the two men.

The Cunard company was the only shipping line on the Atlantic still using paddles, and the relationship between competition and innovation had been a constant discussion point among the Cunard partners, with Samuel Cunard preferring to adopt improvements only after they had been thoroughly tested by someone else. He refused to have this policy changed as he was well aware that an all-year-round trans-Atlantic shipping service was a business where even the most technically sound enterprises, such as the Great Western Steamship Company (1838–46), could founder after adverse publicity resulting from breakdowns and accidents.

Cunard wasn't alone in having reservations about propeller-driven ships at this stage. The Lords of the Admiralty refused to accept evidence of the superiority of the screw, and until 1869 steam in the Navy was used only as an auxiliary to sail.

Towards the end of the 1850s the announcement that a ship to be named the *Great Eastern* was being built in London convinced George Burns more than ever that Cunard's Atlantic supremacy was coming to an end. Designed by Isambard Brunel, one of the greatest British engineers of the Victorian era, the *Great Eastern* was to be almost twice as long as any steamer afloat, with a gross tonnage of 18,914 tons, and she was to be equipped with both paddle-wheels and screw-propellers. Burns told Samuel Cunard that he would retire from shipping for good if they didn't switch to screw-propellers before the *Great Eastern* was launched.

Samuel Cunard stood his ground, and George Burns, finally defeated, retired from business and built himself a home at Wemyss Bay, Ayrshire, on the Firth of Clyde, where he lived to the age of ninety-five. His sons, John Burns, who became the first Lord Inverclyde, and James Cleland Burns, took their place with the Cunard company on his retirement. However, towards the end of his working life, Samuel took less interest in the company, and finally Cunard did commission propeller-driven ships.

The *Great Eastern* was launched in 1859 and, once again, Samuel Cunard's judgement proved right. The ship was a failure as an Atlantic liner. On her first crossing high seas swept away her paddle-wheels, broke the rudder, and knocked over the cow house. A cow fell through a skylight onto the passengers in the saloon and after that first voyage passengers

(*Left*) *The Great Eastern*, designed by Isambard Brunel and launched in 1859, was intended to take over Cunard's Atlantic supremacy. It proved a failure as an Atlantic liner (here pictured at New York).

(*Right, above*) *Scotia*, the last of the Cunard transatlantic paddle ships.

(*Right, below*) *China*, the first screw-propelled Cunard mail ship. She made history by becoming the first Cunarder with accommodation for emigrants to America.

were reluctant to sail in her. The *Great Eastern* finished her days laying the Atlantic telephone cable.

In 1863, at the age of 76, Sir Samuel was himself forced to retire following a heart attack, and Edward replaced his father as the senior partner, making his home in New York and dividing his time between England and America. When the lease on Bush Hill House in north London ran out, Sir Samuel moved with his daughter, Elizabeth, to a large house in Prince's Gate, Kensington, which he had previously occupied. It was here, after he had returned from his last voyage from Halifax, that he suffered a severe attack of bronchitis, and on April 28th, 1865, he died with both his sons, Edward and William, by his bedside. He was 78 years of age.

Sir Samuel Cunard's biographer, Nova-Scotia-born Kay Grant, writing of his last hours in her book *Samuel Cunard – Pioneer of the Atlantic Steamship* (Abelard-Schuman, 1967), tells of how, right up to his death, he regretted never having patched up his quarrel with George Burns.

On the afternoon of the day of his death he asked his son, Edward, to write to his old partner sending his good wishes and regards. The letter,

which George Burns received at his home in Scotland, read:

> My father just now desired me to send his sincerest wishes for your welfare and all your family, and this is the last message, I fear, you will ever receive from him. He thinks himself his hours are numbered . . . He has within the past week spoken of you in the strongest terms of affection, and referred to years long past. Through all the troubles and vexations which afterwards sprang up, he has never ceased to entertain the same regard for you and Mrs Burns and John and Jamie.

After Sir Samuel's death, Edward inherited the title and continued at the head of the company until his own death only four years after his father when the second son, William, took over.

Eventually, the death of the Atlantic paddle-steamer came about. But it took a long time dying as, like Sir Samuel Cunard, the Atlantic travelling public put far more trust in paddles than in propellers. To them, paddle-wheels offered visible reassurance of a ship's power in much the same way as later generations looked upon the number of funnels a ship possessed, and they were unmoved by ships whose screws revolved unseen.

Cunard took delivery of her first screw-propelled Atlantic mail ship, the *China*, in *1862*, and in operation she proved more economical than her paddle-driven contemporary, *Scotia*, burning 82 tons of coal a day for a speed of $12\frac{1}{2}$ knots against *Scotia*'s 164 tons for 14 knots, and her more compact machinery left greater space for cargo. The elimination of the paddle-boxes also enabled passenger cabins to be sited amidships, making them more comfortable. The *China* made history by becoming the first Cunarder with accommodation for emigrants to America; the emigrant trade was going to mean a great deal for Cunard's future.

Sir Samuel Cunard shortly before his death in his London home in 1865 at the age of 78.

CHAPTER FIVE

The Emigrants

As the population of the United States and Canada massively increased during the second half of the 19th century, due mainly to emigration from Britain and Europe, Liverpool became the major passenger port for the poor, the landless and the adventurous, seeking better lives in the New World. Between 1860 and 1900 some 14 million immigrants arrived in America, 80 per cent from Europe, with Liverpool handling about one third of the total. It was one of the greatest movements of people ever known and there was only one way to get there – by ship across the Atlantic.

Emigrants from Britain, Ireland, Sweden, Holland, Germany and Russia all came to Liverpool looking for ships bound for the new lands of promise, and those who didn't get passage to the United States and Canada ventured further afield, many taking ship to the other side of the world to dig for gold in Australia.

At first the sailing packets monopolized the trade, and conditions for the emigrants could not have been much worse. It took up to 35 days to reach America, and up to 4 months to get to Australia, depending on the favourability of winds and frequency of storms. Herded into airless cargo holds where bunks had been set up in tiers, men, women and children slept and lived in conditions where contagious diseases, like typhoid and cholera, went unchecked and spread throughout the ships. Many died at sea on these overcrowded sailing packets and their bodies were thrown overboard. If not enough died on the voyage, which meant unlawful overcrowding would be discovered on reaching America, surplus passengers were dumped at isolated spots on the coast of Newfoundland and many were never heard of again.

Conditions were even worse on ships carrying emigrants fleeing from the tragic Irish famine of the mid-nineteenth century when succeeding crops of potatoes were destroyed by disease. On one emigrant ship alone, 158 passengers died of typhoid and cholera between Liverpool and Quebec.

The cost of steerage passage on the emigrant ships was kept remarkably low because of the competitive nature of the business, and the number of new shipping lines jumping on the band wagon. Despite this and rising costs, the shipping lines continued to make profits helped by the revenue from cabin fares, mails and freight, all of which remained steady throughout most of the rest of the century.

In 1860 it cost £8 8s to cross the Atlantic steerage. By 1863 the fare had 45

Emigrants for America get
their first sight aboard the
Cunarder *Scythia*.

Emigrants for America
arriving at Liverpool Docks
to embark on a Cunard ship.
Gangs of 'runners' awaited
their arrival offering
'assistance'.

Between 1860 and 1900, 14 million immigrants arrived in America, with Liverpool handling one third of the total. This artist's impression shows emigrants boarding a tender for the Cunarder, S.S. *Scythia*, launched in 1875.

come down to £6 6s. After 1883 further fierce competition brought down steerage fares to £4 4s, and it was only in the 1890s that the rates were able to rise to £5. Fares to Australia in the steerage class ranged from £15 to £20.

It was as a direct result of allegations of overcrowding, insanitary conditions and poor food that the British Government was forced to impose controls on the emigrant trade, and in the 1860s an Act came into force to regulate conditions under which passengers could be carried. The Act laid down that not more than one person could be booked per berth apart from husbands and wives and women and children; all unmarried males above the age of twelve had to be accommodated in the fore part of the ship; separate water closets had to be provided for women; ventilation in all passenger quarters had to be of a standard satisfactory to emigration authorities; catering arrangements had to be improved so that it was no longer necessary for passengers to travel with their own store of food for the journey; medical checks on both passengers and crew had to be made before sailing; and ships carrying more than 300 passengers had to have a doctor aboard.

At first it was the Irish who made up the bulk of the emigrants from Liverpool, but the English soon caught them up as the largest national emigrant group, coming mostly from the urban areas and, in the 1880s, from the farming lands; then thousands of small farmers and agricultural workers, their livings ruined by heavy imports of foreign cereals, were forced to leave the country. Poverty, or the fear of poverty, was one of the

More affluent passengers leaving Liverpool on the Cunarder *Scythia*.

strongest motives for families deciding to travel many thousands of miles in search of new lives. In Britain, unemployed industrial workers, many from the cotton mills of Lancashire and the mines of Wales, saw emigration as their only hope of finding work and feeding their families. Ambition was another motive: people looked to emigration as a key which could open doors to a higher life style. These included many whose hopes had been fired by the discovery of gold in California in 1849, and, two years later, in Australia. Fear was a third motive which came about later in the century when thousands of Russian and Polish Jews fled from the discrimination and persecution that was making their lives intolerable. Many of these Eastern Jews passed through Liverpool on their long journey to the United States, having crossed the North Sea to Hull and Grimsby and travelled to Liverpool by train.

As the nineteenth century progressed there were increasing opportunities in industry in the United States. Lancashire cotton workers were attracted to the Massachusetts mill towns, and Welsh miners to Pennsylvania and Ohio. Jews from Eastern Europe congregated in the tenements of New York's Lower East Side, often making clothes in small workshops or in their homes. Construction of the vast trans-continental railways, such as the Union Pacific which opened in 1869, also gave work to thousands of immigrants.

For many the misery of the sea crossing came on top of a period of trouble ashore before joining ship, as most had to spend up to ten days in Liverpool before getting berths. On arrival in the docks area the bewildered emigrant was often approached by gangs of 'runners' who offered to carry luggage and recommend lodging houses, shops and passenger brokers. The lodging

Scenes between decks on an emigrant ship.

An early embarkation scene showing emigrants at Waterloo Docks, Liverpool.

housekeepers, shop owners and brokers paid commission to the runners on each emigrant they brought in and violence awaited all those who refused to pay the exorbitant sums demanded.

Even on reaching the United States trouble for the poor traveller wasn't over. New York was the main arrival port and the dockside scenes in the early days of the emigrant trade were chaotic, with the newly arrived having to run the gauntlet of the American version of the runners, a bunch of confidence tricksters and criminals as notorious as those in Liverpool.

Near the end of the nineteenth century, Ellis Island became the main reception area for immigrants arriving at New York. At Ellis Island the huddled masses of immigrants were not always welcomed with open arms. Medical inspection and questioning by officials was very thorough and those with insufficient money, or certain illnesses, were sent back to

Emigration to the New World was not only for the young. Here aboard the Cunarder *Parthia* senior citizens of the day discuss the future.

Europe. Contract labourers recruited in Europe for a particular job were also excluded as it was believed they were being imported to lower wage standards, or to break strikes.

Few immigrants had employment arranged and, to find work, many faced a further journey from the arrival ports, inland by rail, river steamboat, horse-drawn wagon or on foot. Some were going to join friends and relations, others responding to advertisements seen on arrival or else to general opportunities they had read about before leaving their home shores. In the mid 1870s, Canada, by then a British colony with some degree of self-government, offered assisted passages and free land grants to attract immigrants to populate the prairies.

An advertisement names a fleet of 28 mail steamers appointed by Her Majesty's Postmaster General sailing to New York or Boston. The notice states 'With the view of diminishing the chances of Collision, the Steamers of this Line take a specified course for all seasons of the year.' Single fares cost from 15 to 21 guineas.

As steam replaced sail, the emigration situation both ashore and afloat began to improve and it was not long before representatives of the various steamship companies at Liverpool, including Cunard, began meeting the emigrants on arrival and taking them to respectable lodging houses, thus squeezing out the notorious runners.

Today, the perils faced by emigrants in the nineteenth century can be re-lived in an 'Emigrants to a New World' exhibition at the Merseyside Maritime Museum, Liverpool, opened in 1986. Here, visitors can walk down a reconstructed mid-nineteenth-century Liverpool street, past an emigrant lodging house and ticket office, and then into the reconstructed hold of an emigrant sailing ship to see for themselves the cramped conditions where they slept and lived for weeks at a time. Even sound effects and smells are provided, and on some days there are actors on the ship and in the street performing an emigration drama based on actual events. Visitors will also find an 'Emigration Bureau', an information centre designed to help those who wish to know how to begin tracing the history of their ancestors' journeys to America, Canada and Australia.

The Cunard partners had taken their time to move into the emigrant business, for after Sir Samuel's death the company was without the strong leadership given by its late founder. Sir Samuel's successor, his eldest son, Sir Edward, spent too much of his time in New York; Charles MacIver was getting on in years; and John and Jamie Burns were sadly lacking in experience.

By the time the company took delivery of *China*, the first Cunarder built with accommodation for emigrants, competition for the emigrant trade was already fierce and led by a new British company, the Inman Line. William Inman was a young man of 24 who had started his business life in the Liverpool offices of one of the shipping agencies; in 1850 he set up on his own to compete with Cunard with his first two ships, *City of Glasgow* and the *City of Manchester*, two excellent iron screw steamers, followed by a steady succession of further *City* vessels.

The *City of Glasgow* carried 52 cabin or first-class passengers, 85 second class and 400 steerage emigrants, and became the first trans-Atlantic steamer to carry emigrants direct to the United States whereas, previously, the bulk of the emigrant trade had been carried in the empty 'tween decks of westward bound timber ships to Canadian ports. Inman took passage with his wife on one of the first of his ships across the Atlantic to 'try and ameliorate the discomforts and evil hitherto too common in emigrant ships.'

He seems to have been successful in his mission, for soon after his trip the Inman Line caught on quickly with the emigrant class of passenger, earning a good name for speed and comfort. Unfortunately, the line also earned a reputation for being accident prone: first came the sinking at sea of the *City of Glasgow* with the loss of 480 people in 1854; followed by *City of Philadelphia* (wrecked, 1854); *City of New York* (wrecked, 1864); *City of Boston* (missing, 1870); *City of Washington* (wrecked off Nova Scotia, 1873); *City of Limerick*, (missing, 1881); *City of Brussels* (sunk in 51 collision, Mersey, 1883); and *City of Montreal* (burned at sea, 1887).

Had it not been for this series of tragic events, the Inman Line could have outlasted most of its rivals, but in 1883, after a period of financial depression, Inman sold his business to an American company and it was renamed the Inman and International Steamship Company. In 1893 it changed from its British registry and its ships henceforth sailed under the American flag.

The large financial returns Inman and others made at the start of the emigrant trade had not gone unnoticed and Cunard's entry into the business was joined by three other British Lines, Guion (the Liverpool and Great Western Steamship Company), National and White Star.

Entry into the emigrant trade was not without problems for Cunard. As well as the competition, the American Civil War of the 1860s cut the flow of emigrants and Cunard was forced to suspend the service for a time. But emigration from Liverpool by Cunard went on well into the twentieth century. When the flow of passengers for America began to revive, Cunard needed to build faster and bigger ships to carry steerage emigrants, and re-fit their existing Atlantic fleet. Between 1863 and 1873 the company added some 44,000 gross tons and the cost was high. Mr Henry Knight, who travelled to New York on the *Bothnia* in July 1881, wrote: 'We took more immigrants [*sic*] on board at Queenstown and I went into the steerage to see their accommodation, the cabins are good with two tiers of beds each side and passage down the middle each shelf of beds holding 5 or 6 persons women on one side and men on the other – married people and their families having separate cabins – many of them are very dirty and all seem very poor.'

One of the new screw-steamer replacements for Cunard's Atlantic fleet,

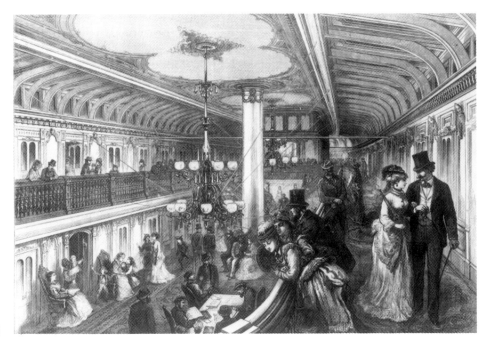

Saloon scene on a steamship.

Emigration by Cunard went on well into the 20th century. These settlers bound for Canada are pictured aboard *Caronia*, launched in 1905.

PARTY OF SETTLERS BOUND FOR CANADA ON BOARD THE CUNARD LINER "CARONIA."

and one of the most famous, was a beautiful ship named the *Russia*, built by J. and G. Thomson, Glasgow, and introduced in 1867. With a clipper bow and clean-cut lines the *Russia* made even the proud tea clippers envious. Internally she was a luxurious, comfortable ship, and she still further cut down the passage time across the Atlantic. On one occasion in 1869 the *Russia* and the famous *City of Paris* of the Inman Line left New York within one hour of each other. For four days these two great ships were in company, but in the end, despite the fact that *Russia* had started last, she arrived in Liverpool 35 minutes ahead of her rival.

A Liverpool-born businessman who sailed to New York in the *Russia* in 1872 wrote an account of the experience in the *Cunard Magazine* some fifty years later and told of an elderly lady passenger remarking to him one day that she always advised her friends to travel in a Cunard steamer 'because they always get there!' Part of his account goes:

As a native of Liverpool I had long looked forward to crossing the Atlantic Ocean, and for me there was only one line of steamers to seek passage for myself and stepson. This was arranged for the sailing of the Cunard liner, *Russia*, on the first Saturday of August, 1872.

We secured a two-berth cabin under the long saloon. She was a beautiful yacht-like craft, of 5,380 tons displacement, barque-rigged, and with a graceful cutwater bowsprit.

We soon settled down, and, after receiving the mails as we went slowly down river off Seacombe, we went ahead in beautiful sunny weather. We put into Queenstown Harbour next day, and took in more mails, passengers, and fresh provisions.

There were several important persons on board, some M.P.s, and a high official of Trinity House. Good weather prevailed for about a week when we encountered a heavy N.W. gale with tremendous billows. The *Russia* took it all with ease, and towered up one wave and down the bottom of another in the most elegant manner, shipping no water. I remember struggling up to the saloon deck early in the morning, and found a rope run to hold on by.

On the crest of a wave one could only see two more beyond it, and each one appeared to be as long as the ship. It was a grand spectacle, the sun shining brightly.

I had an introduction to Captain Cook, but only had a word or two with him at intervals. He kept aloof from his passengers and was a great disciplinarian. I think there were three officers with him, all masters, and fine seamen.

We ran about 320 nautical miles daily. Sails were employed as required. Our appetites were very good, and our food was excellent and varied. We landed in the Company's dock at New York on the tenth morning.

After touring through Canada and California we returned in the *Russia* early in October, and had a pleasant voyage home.

A blow to Cunard's prestige came in 1870 when the White Star Line made Atlantic competition even fiercer with the launching of *Oceanic*, a 17,000-ton ship described as 'the ship which makes possible the concept of a steamship as a travelling palace.' The *Oceanic* had a dining saloon which extended the full width of the ship; state rooms far bigger than any built before; electric bells that summoned stewards at the touch of a finger on an ivory button; water taps instead of water jugs; oil lamps instead of candles; bathtubs and central heating. And, at last, no longer was it necessary to choose between a chamber pot which might slop over with the vessel's motion, and a journey across decks in the middle of the night. Lavatories had been provided near the sleeping accommodation.

Even if the reality of the *Oceanic* was not exactly a palace at sea, the theory of a floating liner-cum-hotel was emerging and the last thirty years of the nineteenth century were to see great progress in the world of shipping. All ships were to be lit by electricity; extra passenger decks amidships were to be incorporated into liners giving additional suites, single cabins, dining saloons and ornate lounges; refrigeration would allow frozen meat and fruit to be transported; sails and yards were to disappear from the masts; bilge keels would give extra seaway stability; twin screws would arrive; three-cylinder engines with triple expansion of the steam would be followed by those with quadruple expansion; and new ship designs with straight stems and more funnels would give new profiles. With each succeeding decade, ships became bigger and faster.

Cunard, once established in the emigration business, had a great deal of leeway to make up, if they were to keep their proud name and match the plans of other companies for sweeping changes in new ships. Luckily, throughout its history, Cunard had been noted for remarkable resilience as well as dependability, and time after time the company has bounced back to confound competitors and critics. Between 1875 and 1880, Cunard's chief competitors, Inman and White Star, began producing bigger and better ships, superior in speed, passenger accommodation and operational efficiency, and Cunard had to do something quickly to reverse the situation. There was serious disagreement, however, among the management of the day on how best this could be achieved.

The austere ways of Samuel Cunard still persisted and some of those at the head of the company he had founded were still resisting demands for more luxurious treatment of passengers. Spartan food and lack of comfort in public rooms – despite the dependability of the service – were no longer acceptable, and many Cunard faithfuls were changing to competitors' lines. The late Francis E. Hyde, a former professor of Economic History at Liverpool University, wrote in his book on the business history of the Cunard company, *Cunard and the North Atlantic: 1840–1973*:

> Small cabins, lack of public rooms, and illumination by candle-light were no match for the attractive features provided for emigrants by the Inman line in the shape of saloons, iced water, set meals and information printed in three languages. It took Cunard a long time to accept such frills – frills which by the 1870s were bringing to cabin class passengers conditions normally experienced in the best hotels of the time. The fact that in the early years Cunard did not offer a high degree of luxury did not usually worry the partners; they treated complaints in a somewhat cavalier fashion. 'Going to sea was a hardship,' wrote Charles MacIver senior to a dissatisfied traveller. 'The Company did not undertake to make anything else out of it.' The innate conservatism in management was also reflected in the maintenance of business methods which had been changed very little over a period of forty years.

Things came to a head in 1878 when the company's finances began to suffer and it became necessary to form a joint-stock company (a limited company), and then go public. Shares in the company were eagerly snapped up by investors and Cunard, under a new house flag – a golden lion wearing an imperial crown, and holding a globe of the world – was once again ready to take on all-comers.

With a new lease of life, and John Burns as the chairman of the new company, it was decided that Cunard should at last start a programme of building bigger and more opulent ships to recapture the high-price Atlantic trade. This new policy decision was not reached easily. The two MacIver brothers who had taken over from their father were not in agreement about the type of ships to be built, but they were no match for the dominant personality of John Burns, who not only won the day but also forced their resignations, which finally, after unfortunate litigation 55

in the High Court, caused a complete break between the MacIver family and the company.

By 1885, Cunard had added eight new ships to their fleet bringing a total tonnage of 53,000 tons, the largest tonnage increase undertaken by a British passenger company in the nineteenth century; the company's original capital of £270,000 had been increased over four-fold. Cunard's leap ahead started with *Servia* (7,392 tons), the first Cunarder to be built of steel, and the first steamship in the world to be lit by electricity, the most welcome of all improvements in ocean liners. *Servia* was the first express passenger ship built to rely solely on passenger revenue derived from fast passages across the Atlantic, and her 10,500 horsepower machinery gave her a speed of $16\frac{1}{2}$ knots. On two decks she had 202 state rooms for 480 first-class passengers; the larger rooms had wardrobes, dressing tables and double beds, en suite rooms being introduced also for the first time.

Between 1881 and 1883 three further large passenger ships followed: *Catalonia* (4,841 tons), *Pavonia* (5,588 tons) and *Cephalonia* (5,517 tons).

From well before the turn of the century many newly built Cunard ships repeated the names of former vessels and they included: *Asia* (II); *Andania* (II); *Alaunia* (II); *Ascania* (II); *Caronia* (II); *Franconia* (II); *Ivernia* (II); *Laurentic* (II); *Laconia* (II); *Mauretania* (II); *Parthia* (II); *Queen Elizabeth* (II); *Samaria* (II); *Sylvania* (II); *Scythia* (II) and *Saxonia* (II).

Some names were even repeated a further time round as in the case of *Aurania* (III) and *Arabia* (III), and since 1895 there have been four

By the 1880s Cunard vessels began to look like steam ships, starting with the *Servia*, the first Cunarder to be built of steel and to be lit by electricity.

The *Servia* was followed by *Catalonia*.

Cephalonia followed *Catalonia*.

Cunard vessels bearing the name *Carinthia*, which has caused a certain amount of confusion ever since, particularly for history researchers. The reason put forward, however, was that it was felt the names of many Cunard vessels which had distinguished themselves should be perpetuated.

In 1883, *Aurania* (7,268 tons) took a role of catering exclusively for the wealthy and the aristocracy, having suites of accommodation and thirteen marble bathrooms. In 1884 came *Etruria* (8,128 tons) and *Umbria* (8,120 tons), the first Cunard vessels to have refrigeration machinery installed and outclassed all their rivals in size and capacity. Last of the series was *Oregon* (7,375 tons), which was built for the Guion line in 1884 to try and outstrip all competition. When Guion ran into financial difficulties and could not meet the building bills, Cunard stepped in and took over the ship, which was immediately to regain for Cunard the trans-Atlantic speed record.

Unfortunately, in the early hours of March 14th, 1886, as *Oregon* was approaching New York and off Fire Island, she was struck amidships by the schooner *Charles H. Morse*. Carrying a heavy cargo of coal, the schooner cut two 20-foot holes into the Oregon's side. It took ten hours for the *Oregon* to sink but not before all 896 passengers and crew had been safely transferred to rescue vessels. Some 464 bags of mail were also safely

salvaged, having been washed up along the coast from Portland to Cape Hatteras. The sinking of the *Oregon* was by then only the second peacetime loss for Cunard.

Well before the end of the century the steamship had truly come of age; the last auxiliary sail was being discarded; steel was taking the place of iron in hull construction; and propelling machinery was becoming more reliable. There was only one way for Cunard to go – to build even bigger and faster ships.

In 1893, the Fairfield Company of Glasgow built the first two twin-screw Cunarders, *Campania* and *Lucania*, both of 12,950 tons. They were record-breakers from the start and their service speed of 21 knots made them the fastest Atlantic liners of their day. Indeed, their first challenger did not come until 1897 when Norddeutscher Lloyd introduced the *Kaiser Wilhelm der Grosse*, which carried the unprecedented number of 2,300 passengers, and became the fastest liner afloat.

It was in *Lucania* (destroyed by fire in Liverpool in 1910) that Signor Marconi carried out many of his early experiments in wireless transmission in 1901, experiments that led to the publication on board *Lucania* of the first ship's newspaper to appear daily with news received by wireless. *Lucania* was also one of the first Atlantic liners to be built with single berth

Campania shows her speed as she heads towards America shortly after her launching in 1893.

Lucania – a two-bunk cabin.

Lucania, the library.

Lucania: saloon with piano.

Lucania: the dining room.

cabins, and with suites – cabins in pairs with a sitting room between them. She was the first vessel to have coal-burning firegrates in all the principal rooms. She represented a new standard of opulence in first-class accommodation with rooms described in Cunard brochures as suggesting 'the stately chambers of a palace rather than accommodation within the steel walls of a ship'.

The Persian-carpeted drawing room was a splendid room some 60 feet by 30 feet with walls of satinwood, relieved with cedar mouldings, and a ceiling of old ivory and gilding. The settees, ottomans and chairs were upholstered in rich velvets and brocades. A grand piano and an American organ were also provided. Second-class passengers had a drawing room with a cottage piano. There were some who thought that Cunard had gone a little too far with its geraniums blooming in the ladies' room, and its Italian-style dining room with heavy coffered ceilings in white and gold, supported by Ionic columns and richly carved Spanish mahogany walls.

But when the wind of change blew through the Cunard board room nothing was ever done by halves, and the age of the greatest passenger liners ever known was about to dawn – ocean liners designed to satisfy the demands of the rich new travelling public who believed that 'how you travel is who you are'. Of the five major British lines engaged in the passenger and cargo trade across the Atlantic in the second half of the nineteenth century, only Cunard managed to survive into the twentieth.

John Burns also survived to see the start of the new century, but not for long. He died in February 1901, after serving as Cunard's second chairman for 21 years.

PART TWO

1900-1946

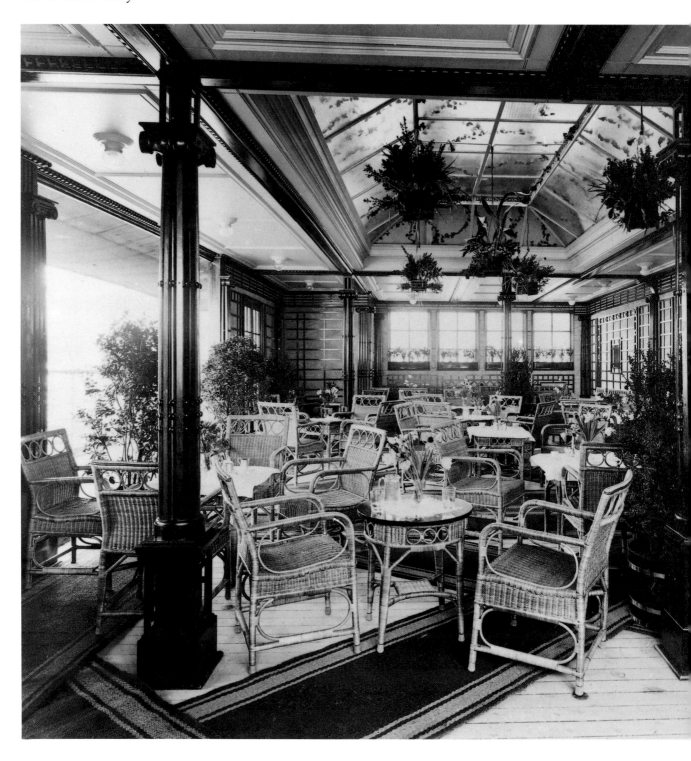

Mauretania: the café.

(*Previous page*) The *Queen Mary* arrives at New York after her maiden voyage.

CHAPTER·SIX

The 'Grand Hotels' at Sea

Cunard may not have been the first to introduce luxury at sea, but when they decided to do so they did it with such an extravagance of grandeur, opulence and style that most of their rivals were put in the shade. In 1907 two giant new four-funnelled ships, the first Cunard Express Liners – *Lusitania*, as long as the Houses of Parliament and *Mauretania*, the latest of the 'greatest steamships the world has ever seen' – became the first 'Grand Hotels' at sea, complete with Palm Courts, orchestras, à la carte restaurants, electric lifts, telephones, and even a daily newspaper printed at sea.

These were the first of the new style of passenger ship – speedy and reliable and carrying the rich and the famous in luxury hotel-style comfort; the first of the big British liners to be powered by turbine engines; and the first to focus world interest and excitement on the Atlantic speed contest.

Lusitania (31,550 tons) preceded *Mauretania* (31,937 tons) by a matter of only months. And, but for the tragedy which shook the world in 1915 when '*Lucy*', as she was affectionately known, was torpedoed off the Irish coast by a German U-boat, causing the loss of 1,198 lives, this great liner could have gone on to become equally famous as a living ship as she was as an underwater tomb for the innocent victims of war, some 300 feet down off the Old Head of Kinsale, Ireland.

Negotiations for building *Mauretania* and *Lusitania*, started by the second Lord Inverclyde, the company's fourth chairman, had gone on for many months before Prime Minister Arthur Balfour made public the terms of the agreement for a government loan during a speech delivered at the Cutler's Feast in Sheffield on September 30th, 1902.

It was a remarkable agreement, mainly brought about by national concern over the growing supremacy of German shipping lines on the Atlantic, particularly the Norddeutscher Lloyd Company with its giant liner, the *Kaiser Wilhelm der Grosse*, which at the turn of the century began beating all records for the Atlantic crossing, outpacing the four Cunard ships then maintaining the line's New York service; it was followed by the Hamburg–America Line launching their *Deutchland* (16,502 tons), a vessel which quickly outpaced the *Kaiser Wilhelm der Grosse*. Another factor was fear that a huge new American shipping combine, the International Mercantile Marine Company, was about to buy up Cunard and deny the British Government the use of the Cunard fleet in time of war. Headed by J. Pierpoint Morgan, the banker and 63 railroad financier, the International Mercantile Marine Company, with a capital of £34,000,000, aimed to gain control of every single steamer line on the North Atlantic and by 1902 it had added the share capitals of the British White Star Line, and the Dominion and Leyland Lines, to the clutch of American lines already owned by them.

Fortuitously, Cunard managed to stay outside the combine and the Morgan threat helped the company obtain a vast government loan of £2,600,000 at only 2¾ per cent interest over 20 years, and an additional Admiralty subsidy of £150,000 per annum as soon as the *Lusitania* and *Mauretania* were built.

This new government agreement with Cunard which came into effect in 1903 stipulated that the line should remain entirely under British control and that under no circumstances should the management of the company be in the hands of, or any shares in the company held by, other than British subjects. Furthermore, it was laid down that both the *Lusitania* and *Mauretania* should be constructed not only to be high-speed passenger liners, but also to be convertible to the requirements of the Admiralty as auxiliary armed cruisers in time of war, and that Cunard was to hold at the disposal of the government the whole of its fleet for hire or purchase on terms agreed during the currency of the agreement. Any plans for new vessels to be built of 17 knots speed and over should also be first submitted to the Admiralty for approval.

In August 1903 Cunard directors decided to refer the vital decision as to whether or not the *Lusitania* and *Mauretania* should be turbine powered to a commission chaired by Mr James Rain (general superintendent of the Cunard Company); it included Rear-Admiral H.J. Oram (representing the Admiralty); Sir William H. White (Swan, Hunter and Wigham Richardson), Mr Andrew Laing (Wallsend Slipway Company), the Hon. C.A. Parsons, C.B. (Parsons Marine Turbine Co.), Mr J.T. Milton (Lloyds Register), Mr Thomas Bell (John Brown and Co.), and Mr William Brock (Denny Brothers).

The commission unanimously reported in favour of the adoption of marine steam turbines on the Parsons principle, the system devised by the Hon. C.A. Parsons, inventor and engineer, later to become Sir Charles Algernon Parsons. The son of the third Earl of Rosse, Charles Parsons, constructed the first turbine vessel, the *Turbinia*, a little craft of 44 tons which appeared at the Spithead Naval Review in 1897, held to celebrate the Diamond Jubilee of Queen Victoria, and amazed and delighted spectators by dashing in and out of the assembled Royal Navy fleet attaining a speed of 34.5 knots, a new record.

In advance of building the two 700-foot-long giants, *Lusitania* and *Mauretania*, Cunard launched in 1905 two ships which became known as 'The Pretty Sisters', *Caronia*, 19,687 tons, and *Carmania*, 19,524 tons. It was in *Carmania* that a high-powered turbine system was tried out in preparation for the Parsons turbines in the projected express liners. The *Caronia* made history by being the first Atlantic liner fitted, for safety purposes, with a system of watertight doors that could be operated simul-

(From left to right from top) Laconia; Berengaria 'the largest liner in commission in the world'; loading freight in Cunard steamers at Liverpool Docks; *Carmania* – the other half of the 'pretty sisters' team, which took part in one of the classic sea battles of the First World War; cigarette card of *Britannia.*

CHURCHMAN'S
CIGARETTES

(From left to right from top)
Mauretania; Aquitania;
first-class swimming bath on
the *Olympic*; second-class
state room on the *Olympic*.

taneously from a central control on the bridge. Both these huge experimental ships, with speeds of 18 knots and capable of carrying 10,000 tons of cargo and coal and about 2,600 passengers, were highly successful.

So, at the turn of the century, Cunard, having successfully overcome a crisis in both political and financial terms, emerged as the premier British passenger line, secure in its position, and recognized by the government as a national asset. Unfortunately, the second Lord Inverclyde did not live to see the results of his labours and foresight materialize. At the yard of John Brown on Clydebank he performed the ceremony of driving the first rivet into the hull of *Lusitania* and died a year later. *Lusitania* was named and launched by his widow, Mary, Lady Inverclyde, when Cunard's new chairman, Mr William Watson, told the watching crowds that Lady Inverclyde, at considerable cost to her feelings, had agreed to launch *Lusitania* to honour the memory of her husband. The link had finally been broken between Cunard and the original three founder directors.

Interior decoration of the two liners had been one of the top priorities of Cunard directors, and before his death Lord Inverclyde, the last of the Burns family to be part of Cunard's management team, insisted that the finest architects of the day should be commissioned. It was a wise move, for there had been much criticism of the standard of comfort aboard British liners of the time compared with the ornate interiors of American and German ships, the latter sometimes sumptuous to the point of being garish. Even Sir Charles Allom, responsible for interiors at Buckingham Palace, went on record as saying: 'There has been a loss of opportunities to bring ship decoration up to the standard of the improved taste of the last few years.'

Cunard were determined to put the record straight and in 1905, the Scottish architect responsible for the Glasgow Exhibition of 1901, James Millar, was chosen to decorate *Lusitania*, and Harold A. Peto, well known for his country house interior decoration work in Britain, was commissioned to decorate *Mauretania*. Both architects chose the much admired 'period' treatment of the day.

Lusitania's first-class dining saloon, built on two decks with a domed gallery, was clad throughout in white-painted panelling in the Louis XVI style, carved by John Crawford of Glasgow, and gilded by Waring and Gillow. The first-class lounge was panelled in inlaid mahogany in the Georgian style and upholstered with green carpets and furnishings supplied by Waring and Gillow. An Edwardian glass skylight contained twelve panes of stained glass designed by Oscar Patterson, each representing a month of the year, and massive marble fireplaces were at each end of the room overhung with enamel panels by Alexander Fisher. There was a Queen Anne smoking room and an Adamesque writing room.

Peto went to work on *Mauretania* with ingenuity and flourish. The Louis XVI first-class lounge was panelled in acajou moucheté mahogany with columns and fleur-de-pêche marble pilasters disguising the ship's structural elements, while three large French tapestries adorned the walls. The Italian Renaissance walnut smoking room had basket grates

(*Left*) *Mauretania*: first-class smoke room.

(*Right*) A cabin in the *Lusitania*.

The first *Mauretania* (1907).

and fire dogs copied from originals in the Palazzo Varesi and at each end of a plasterwork freize over the cornice hung a picture representing old New York and old Liverpool. The first-class dining room was panelled in straw-coloured Austrian oak in the style of François I with a gold dome that hid electric lamps throwing light against a gilded convex disc and filling the room with a soft glow.

The steam turbines were also responsible for providing greater comfort for passengers. Hitherto, in all steam-driven vessels travelling at high speed, there was much vibration which caused passengers almost as much discomfort as the rolling and pitching of the sea. Vibration had a wearing effect on the machinery generally, and, in rough seas, when the propeller lifted out of the water, the screw raced at double its normal rate, which not only created a disagreeable motion for passengers but caused severe strain on the engines. In a turbine-driven vessel, as well as the absence of vibration, there was no racing and practically no loss of speed because propellers were obliquely set deeper in the water.

When the *Lusitania* and *Mauretania* came into service both ships broke all existing speed records with their revolutionary steam turbine machinery and quadruple-bladed propellers. The British shipping world heaved a huge sigh of relief when the fastest Atlantic crossing was regained first by *Lusitania* steaming 2,781 miles in 4 days, 19 hours and 52 minutes at an average rate of 24 knots, and then by *Mauretania* which attained the marvellous average speed of $27\frac{1}{2}$ knots and crossed the Atlantic in 4 days, 10 hours and 41 minutes. *Mauretania* went on to become the greatest of the Blue Riband holders with unbeaten speeds for 21 years, a legend in her time, and a ship which inspired affection and praise in all who travelled in her.

Franklin D. Roosevelt, known to have disliked travelling by sea, went on record as praising *Mauretania* not only as a ship with a soul, but one that you could talk to. And her Master, Captain Rostron, said of her: 'She has the manners and deportment of a great lady and has behaved herself as such.'

Theodore Dreiser wrote of a voyage in *Mauretania*:

There were several things about this great ship that were unique. It was a beautiful thing all told – its long cherry-wood panelled halls, its heavy porcelain baths, its dainty state rooms fitted with lamps, bureaus, writing desks, wash-stands, closets and the like. I liked the idea of dressing for dinner and seeing everything quite stately and formal. The little be-buttoned callboys in their tight-fitting blue suits amused me. And the bugler who bugled for dinner! That was a most musical sound he made, trilling the various quarters gaily as much as to say, 'This is a very joyous event, ladies and gentlemen. We are all happy; come, come; it is a delightful feast.'

It took a crew of between 800 and 900 to run each of Cunard's new express liners and cater for the 2,300 passengers when fully booked. To

The sparse interior of a third-class cabin on *Lusitania* or *Mauretania*.

Mauretania: the pantry.

power the giants across the Atlantic the 192 furnaces required the constant attention of 204 firemen, working in watches of four hours each, as they shovelled 1,320 tons of coal per day into the blazing fires. Then there were the trimmers employed to see that the 6,600 tons of coal carried aboard each trip was kept in position in the bunkers, and to wheel supplies to the furnace doors.

The navigating staff consisted of the captain, six officers, forty seamen, and a score of men ranging from six quartermasters to a lamp trimmer. Then there were the seamen employed keeping the decks spick and span, seeing that the lifeboats were in order, and manning the 'look-out' in the crow's nest from where they constantly watched out for icebergs when on North Atlantic courses and telephoned the officer on the bridge if any were sighted. A Private Branch Telephone Exchange, the first fitted in an ocean-going steamer, was installed in the *Mauretania*, and connected to first-class staterooms, and in the cabins of the ship's chief doctor, purser and chief steward.

72   More than 350 stewards and a dozen stewardesses were employed to look

after the passengers' every need, and in the kitchens and stores a vast number of chefs, cooks and porters were busy day and night. Before commencing a voyage *Lusitania* and *Mauretania* would each take into store 40 tons of potatoes; 4,000 lb. of fresh fish; 200 boxes dried fish; 40,000 eggs; and 2,000 head of poultry. To supply meat and bacon used up a herd of 40 oxen, a flock of 100 sheep, a drove of 130 pigs, and large quantities of game according to season.

A purser and staff, responsible for the ship's accounts and passengers' bills, made up the rest of the crew, together with a medical team of doctors, sick berth attendants and sick berth stewardesses, always carried to attend sick passengers and crew, and take responsibility for sanitary conditions aboard.

The Shipbuilder, the quarterly magazine of the time devoted to shipbuilding, described the launching of *Lusitania* on June 7th, 1906, in the following words:

Transcending in interest every event of the kind for many years, if not in the entire annals of shipbuilding on the Clyde, the launch of the Cunard liner, *Lusitania*, from the stocks of the Clydebank shipbuilding establishment of Messrs John Brown and Co. Ltd., attracted almost universal attention, and was observed by a vast concourse of spectators, drawn not only from local shipping circles, but from associated sources throughout the kingdom and abroad.

The launch and the coming advent of this triumph in marine architecture must undoubtedly mark an epoch in the development of the steamship, and it is peculiarly appropriate that they should signalise the centenary of practical steam navigation. The *Lusitania* and her sister ship, *Mauretania*, which will follow her from the stocks of Messrs Swan, Hunter, and Wigham Richardson, on the Tyne in September, are expected to steam two miles faster than any of their predecessors in the Atlantic – an increase at one step which involves an addition of about 70 per cent to the 40,000 indicated horse-power developed by the fastest of merchant steamers now afloat.

Not only are they the largest, most powerful, and, by intention, the fastest ocean liners ever constructed, but they are specially interesting and significant as factors in technical development because of the adoption of quadruple screws, and of the turbine system of propulsion in a much more comprehensive form than in any preceding steamships.

In the continuing saga of supremacy of the Atlantic someone, sooner or later, was bound to come up with an answer to Cunard's new 'Big Two'. It came sooner, and within four years of the arrival of *Lusitania* and *Mauretania*, the White Star Line produced *Olympic* and *Titanic*, about half as big again as the Cunarders in terms of gross tonnage. At first White Star had toyed with the idea of going for high speed to catch up with 73

A suite in the *Lusitania*.

Cunard but eventually came down on the side of high living, and when *Olympic* and *Titanic* were launched both ships were more luxurious than anything previously seen afloat, though not as fast as *Lusitania* and *Mauretania*. *Olympic* sailed on her maiden voyage from the Ocean Dock at Southampton on June 14th, 1911, and arrived at the White Star Line's Chelsea Piers off the foot of West 19th Street, New York, in 5 days, 16 hours and 45 minutes.

Many passengers, both British and American, were content to sacrifice speed for the extra luxury time aboard, and, in the *Olympic*, a new-style Extra Tariff Restaurant serviced by Italian and French staff from Oddenino's Imperial Restaurant in London and christened the à la Carte proved so popular that within a year it had to be enlarged to half again its original size.

For the *Titanic*, disaster came on April 14th, 1912. Three days out of Southampton on her maiden voyage to New York, she struck a floating mass of ice at twenty minutes before midnight. The damage caused by the collision with the iceberg extended underwater from the bow as far aft as No. 5 boiler room. With so many compartments laid open to the sea, the fate of the vessel was sealed, and the great 'unsinkable' ship sank 3 hours after the collision. Of the 2,206 persons aboard, only 703 were saved, being picked up by the Cunard *Carpathia* (13,564 tons), one of the first to answer *Titanic*'s distress signal.

The Marconi wireless operator on the *Carpathia*, Harold Cottam, played an important part in helping to get his ship to the rescue of *Titanic* survivors. On the night of the sinking, *Carpathia* was en route from New York to Gibraltar and Genoa and Cottam had exchanged frequent messages with the *Titanic* and other ships. According to the account he gave in later years, Cottam was about to go to bed when he heard a wireless call from Cape Cod telling the *Titanic* there was ice about. Knowing Phillips, the wireless operator of the Titanic, he radioed him to ask if they had heard the call from Cape Cod.

The answer came back, 'We have struck ice, come at once.' The *Carpathia* was then 58 miles from the *Titanic* and travelling in the opposite direction. Cottam asked the *Titanic*'s radio operator whether he should have the *Carpathia* turned round and was told, 'Yes'. He ran up to the bridge, but he could not get the officers to listen, as wireless was a new thing. He then ran to wake his captain, asleep in his cabin. Immediately Captain Rostron heard what his wireless operator had to say he gave orders for *Carpathia* to turn around and make all speed for the *Titanic*'s last position.

The ordinary speed of the *Carpathia* was 14 knots, but that night she made $17\frac{1}{2}$ knots, at the same time keeping a close watch for icebergs. Cottam returned to his radio and remained in touch with the *Titanic* to help her communicate with other vessels in the vicinity as the escape of steam in the stricken liner made it difficult for the operator to hear signals coming in. By the time *Carpathia* reached the scene, in about three hours, the *Titanic* had sunk, but the *Carpathia* was able to pick up 703 survivors

The Palladian lounge in
Aquitania.

and take them to New York.

Among passengers who went to their deaths were Colonel J.J. Astor, the American soldier and inventor; Jacques Futrelle, the American novelist and dramatist; F.D. Millet, the artist; W.T. Stead, the British editor and journalist; and Harry Widener, the millionaire book-collector. The disaster led to the 1913 International Convention for the Safety of Life at Sea. Out of this came the famous International Ice Patrol, sponsored by several nations, and the introduction of improvements in life-saving equipment with boat-drill for passengers becoming a necessary routine.

Captain Arthur Rostron, knighted in 1926, fourteen years after the *Titanic* disaster, became one of the most decorated captains in the world. In America he was conferred with the freedom of New York and decorated with the Congressional Medal of Honour. He also received the French Legion of Honour; the C.B.E. for special war services; the South African Transport Medal for troop carrying during the Boer War; and many medals including one from the Liverpool Shipwreck and Humane Society presented to him by the then Earl of Derby.

Born in Bolton, Lancashire, Rostron started his sea life on the cadet ship *Conway* moored in the Mersey, and was one of the many 'Conway boys' who have gained honour in the profession of the British Mercantile Marine. He joined Cunard as fourth officer on the *Umbria* at the age of twenty-six and later his commands included the *Carpathia*, *Caronia*, *Saxonia*, *Mauretania*, *Berengaria*, *Carmania* and *Andania*.

Typical of many great sailors, retiring, modest, and reluctant to talk of his past, Sir Arthur Rostron, did, however, go on record as saying of the *Titanic* disaster and the part his ship, *Carpathia*, played, 'When we received the S.O.S. we were sixty miles away from the sinking ship. We steamed at full speed and did what we could. It was terrible. I don't like to dwell on the awful scenes. I would say this only, the commander of the *Titanic* was a courageous man, who was blamed unjustly and unnecessarily.'

Shortly before the outbreak of the First World War, both the White Star Line and the Hamburg–America Line had begun introducing liners of over 40,000 tons; Cunard promptly replied by laying down (building the hull) one of the most beautiful ships of all, *Aquitania*, at 45,000 tons, and buying up the shares of the Glasgow-based Anchor Line. *Aquitania*, launched by the Countess of Derby in April 1913, had a Caroline smoking room, an Elizabethan grill room, a Louis XIV dining room, and a Palladian lounge, while the swimming pool was inspired by Egyptian architecture in the British Museum and flanked by fluted columns.

A Cunard publicist wrote of *Aquitania* after her maiden voyage:

The passenger lists tend slightly towards Burke and Debrett. The country family sort of atmosphere. If a ship may be like a house, *Aquitania* is like some Georgian house of weathered brick that looks

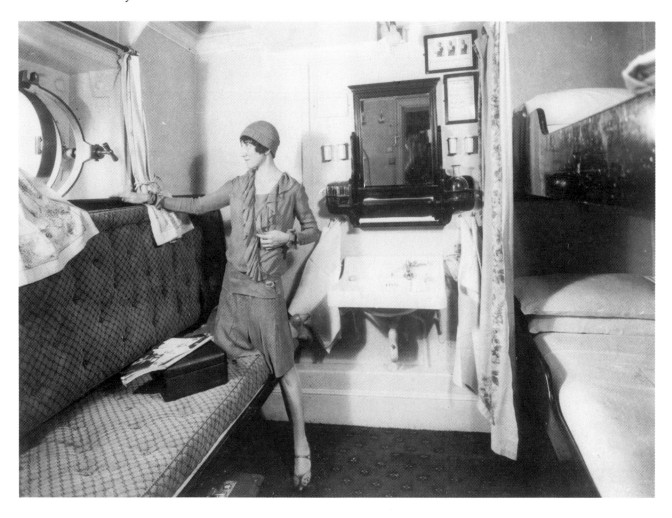

(*Above*) Second-class outside state room in *Aquitania*.

(*Left*) Third-class berths in *Aquitania*.

Aquitania: kitchen.

Aquitania: still room.

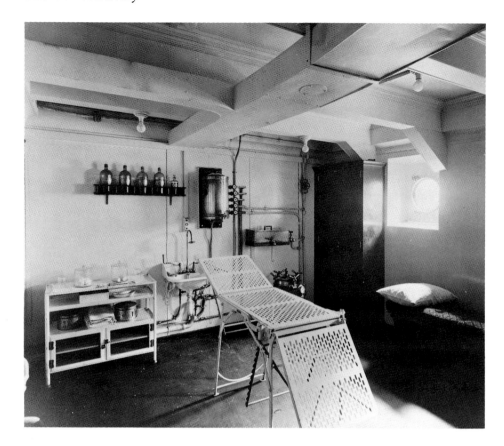

through the mist towards the fairy tale outlines of Windsor Castle. By day, Harris tweed . . . Chanel jerseys . . . indolent conversation, and energetic sport. By night a sudden increase in tempo . . . a blaze of jewels . . . the gleam of ivory shoulders . . . gowns, rose, gold, green . . . men and women both wearing formality brilliance with the perfect ease that is the distinction and delight of aristocratic English life.

For many years *Mauretania* and *Aquitania* were the pride and joy of Cunard. *Aquitania* did not go to the breakers until she had completed 35 years continuous service, served in 2 major wars, steamed 3 million miles, and carried 1,200,000 passengers. When *Mauretania* was steaming on the way to the breaker's yard she signalled the men who built her at Swan, Hunter and Wigham Richardson: 'Goodbye, Tyneside. This is my last radio. Closing down for ever. *Mauretania*.' As she came up to her last berth at Rosyth a piper on the dockside played the lament, 'Flowers of the Forest'. There was one further tribute. On her way up the Forth *Mauretania* was hailed by a small outward bound tramp ship: 'Good-bye old lady, it's a damn shame.'

CHAPTER SEVEN

The First World War: No Holds Barred

On the outbreak of war Cunard's normal commercial activities had become severely dislocated, as the 1903 agreement gave the government the right to take over most of Cunard's ships in time of war as armed cruisers, troop transports, hospital or prison ships. Faced with the dilemma of fulfilling their obligations, and at the same time continuing some semblance of service for the carriage of passengers, the board of Cunard took the decision, with Admiralty approval, to retain *Lusitania* in the company's employment and use her for normal commercial work until required otherwise.

So, weeks before *Lusitania* sailed from New York on her last voyage, the time and date of her departure had been regularly advertised in American newspapers as though everything was peaceful. However, on the morning of May 1st, 1915, as *Lusitania* left Cunard Pier into the Hudson River and headed down harbour past the Statue of Liberty, a more ominous form of advertisement appeared in the American press. Issued on behalf of the Imperial German Embassy in Washington, it read:

> Travellers intending to embark on the Atlantic voyage are reminded that a state of war exists between Germany and her allies, and Great Britain and her allies; that the zone of war includes the waters adjacent to the British Isles; that, in accordance with formal notice given by the Imperial German Government, vessels flying the flag of Great Britain, or any of her allies, are liable to destruction in those waters and that travellers sailing in the war zone on ships of Great Britain or her allies do so at their own risk.

Some individual passengers had also received warnings in the form of anonymous telegrams. One sent to Alfred G. Vanderbilt, the American millionaire, read:

HAVE IT ON DEFINITE AUTHORITY THE LUSITANIA IS TO BE TORPEDOED. YOU HAD BETTER CANCEL PASSAGE IMMEDIATELY. SIGNED: MORTE.

None of the warnings resulted in passenger cancellations and Alfred G. Vanderbilt told newspaper men before he sailed: 'Why should we be afraid of German submarines? We can outdistance any submarine afloat.' It was interesting to note that Americans were already looking upon the fame of Cunard liners as part of the American heritage.

There had been no secret about the time of the *Lusitania*'s sailing from New York for Liverpool. Britain was still under the delusion that Germany would never dare sink an unarmed liner carrying civilian passengers and would honour the gentleman's code of war; the Admiralty had even discounted as a bluff the German declaration that all vessels flying the flag of Great Britain, or any of her allies, were liable in future to destruction. The Admiralty appeared so confident that nothing would happen to the *Lusitania* that they even withdrew the usual naval escort for the last leg of the journey.

But was *Lusitania* only an unarmed passenger liner? Germany could well have thought otherwise, for the country's pre-war spies in Britain would have been failing in their duties if they hadn't discovered some details of the special Admiralty specifications for both *Lusitania* and *Mauretania*, which stated:

In getting out the design, special attention must be paid to the stability. The ship must be as steady as possible under the varying conditions to which a ship of the high speed defined in the contract would be subjected in the North Atlantic Trade, and the stability should be so arranged that, by the use of water ballast, the ship may have a positive metacentic height in the worst condition when fitted as an armed cruiser.

Foundations for gun platforms to be fitted as per special agreement to be made with the British Government; spaces for gun ports and magazines to be arranged for. Decks to be stiffened in way of gun positions, if so required.

The armament contemplated for each of these vessels consists of twelve six-inch guns of the latest type, and a number of lighter guns of a type not yet settled.

Gun positions with suitable supports worked into the ship will be required for the six-inch guns, four on the forecastle, six on the shelter decks amidships, and two on the shelter deck right aft. The clear space for working the six-inch guns to have a radius of thirteen feet from the axis of training of the gun, with a minimum training from sixty degrees before to sixty degrees abaft the beam for the broadside guns.

Sketches of the proposed positions for the six-inch guns and the nature of the supports should be prepared by the Builders in conjunction with the Admiralty Inspecting Officer for submission to the Admiralty at an early stage of the design.

The magazines for service when the vessel is employed as a cruiser will require to be below the waterline in the extreme forward and after holds, and it is desirable that these spaces should be covered by a steel deck and provided with arrangements for rapidly flooding them in the event of fire in the adjacent compartments.

A sketch of the course of ammunition from the magazines to the guns should be prepared, with a statement of the facilities for lifting and transporting the ammunition.

(*Right*) *Mauretania* – complete with Palm Court, electric lifts, telephones and even a daily newspaper printed at sea. Painting by Montague Davison.

(*Right, below*) The Cunard fleet, including *Queen Elizabeth, Queen Mary, Mauretania, Caronia, Britannic, Media, Parthia, Carinthia, Ivernia, Saxonia, Sylvania* and *Scythia*.

EMBARKATION · NOTICE

SAILINGS FROM SOUTHAMPTON

STEAMER	TO	SPECIAL TRAIN FROM WATERLOO STATION, LONDON.		PASSENGERS EMBARK WITH BAGGAGE.	
LANCASTRIA	HALIFAX, N.S. and NEW YORK (Via Cherbourg) SATURDAY, DEC. 1st, 1928	Cabin 10-20 a.m	Tourist T/C 10-20 a.m.	Cabin 12-00 noon	Tourist T/C 11-00 a.m.
BERENGARIA	NEW YORK (Via Cherbourg) WEDNESDAY, DEC. 5th, 1928	First Class 8-15 p.m. Tuesday, Dec. 4th	Second Class and Tourist T/C 3-45 p.m. Tuesday, Dec. 4th	First Class 6-0 p.m. Tuesday, Dec. 4th	Second Class 6-00 p.m. Tourist T/C 5-00 p.m. Tuesday, Dec. 4th
AURANIA - -	HALIFAX, N.S. and NEW YORK (Via Cherbourg) THURSDAY, DEC. 6th, 1928	Cabin 10-20 a.m.	Tourist T/C 10-20 a.m.	Cabin 12-00 Noon.	Tourist T/C 11-00 a.m
CARONIA - -	HALIFAX, N.S. and NEW YORK (Via Cherbourg) FRIDAY, DEC. 14th, 1928	Cabin 10-20 a.m.	Tourist T/C 10-20 a.m.	Cabin 12-00 noon.	Tourist T/C 11-00 a.m.
AUSONIA - -	HALIFAX, N.S. and NEW YORK (Via Cherbourg) THURSDAY, DEC. 20th, 1928	Cabin 10-20 a.m.	Tourist T/C 10-20 a.m.	Cabin 12-00 Noon.	Tourist T/C 11-00 a.m.
BERENGARIA	NEW YORK (Via Cherbourg) THURSDAY, DEC. 27th, 1928	First Class 8-50 a.m.	Second Class and Tourist T/C 8-10 a.m.	First Class 11-00 a.m.	Second Class 10-00 a.m. Tourist T/C 9-00 a.m.

FOR FURTHER PARTICULARS RE EMBARKATION AND RESERVATIONS FOR SPECIAL TRAINS, SEE OVER.

CUNARD · LINE

(*Above*) An artist's impression of the sinking of the *Lusitania*.

(*Left*) Cunard embarkation notice for 1928.

Both *Lusitania* and *Mauretania* had, by the 1903 government agreement, been built specifically for quick conversion into heavily armed fast merchant cruisers, and could have easily become potential menaces to an enemy.

There was no disputing, of course, that Cunard had made it perfectly clear that the *Lusitania*, at the time of her last fatal voyage, was acting only as a passenger liner. Furthermore, none of the survivors, passengers or crew, ever reported seeing guns mounted on the ship. But it did not help matters when it was discovered after the sinking that, as well as passengers, *Lusitania* had carried among her declared cargo, 4,200 cases of small arms ammunition and 1,259 cases of steel shrapnel shells, plus 3,863 boxes of cheese and 696 tubs of butter destined for the Naval Experimental Establishment at Shoeburyness, and that all cargo holds had been commandeered by the Admiralty.

On the afternoon of Friday, May 7th, 1915, ten miles off the southern shores of Ireland, abeam of the Old Head of Kinsale, a German U-20 submarine was lurking six fathoms below the surface in the main shipping route to the St George's Channel. Captain Walter Schweiger had been waiting for his next victim. Seven days out of Emden, the U-20 had already sunk three British merchant vessels, a schooner and two steamers, in the same waters, and the Kapitanleutnant was down to his last two G-type torpedoes.

There was hope that the next victim was going to be the biggest and best, for shortly before submerging a large steamer had been sighted through binoculars approaching from the distant west, and Schweiger had given the order, 'Diving stations'. It was only when the big steamer came within periscope vision that Kapitanleutnant Schweiger realized just how big his prize target was going to be.

It was a 762-foot long passenger liner with four raked funnels set on a white gleaming superstructure and painted in the Cunard livery (funnels, bright red with black top; hull, black; uppers, white; masts, buff; lifeboats, white.) It could only be the *Lusitania*, for she was the sole liner of that size on the trans-Atlantic service at the time. The U-20 fired one torpedo at 2,000 yards in perfect conditions for a hit. The torpedo struck the liner amidships on her starboard side, and exploded. A second explosion followed inside the hull, forward of the first funnel, destroying the bulkheads of her watertight compartments. Within twenty minutes the *Lusitania* had plunged to the bottom. The reason for the second explosion, which allowed thousands of tons of water to enter the vessel, is still a matter for conjecture today.

Out of nearly 2,000 people aboard, only 761 survived, picked up by rescue craft. Of the 159 Americans, 124 perished, including the millionaire, Alfred G. Vanderbilt.

Commodore Sir James Bisset K.T., C.B.E., Captain of the *Queen Mary* and *Queen Elizabeth* during the Second World War, was serving in H.M.S. *Caronia* which rendezvoused with the *Lusitania* outside the territorial waters of New York as she started on her fatal voyage. Sir James, in the third volume of his book, *Commodore*, written in collaboration with P.R. Stephenson (Angus and Robertson, 1961), tells what he saw from the deck of the former Cunarder requisitioned by the Admiralty as an armed merchant cruiser in 1914.

On the bridge of the *Lusitania* I could see her Master, Captain Will Turner, and his Staff Captain, 'Jock' Anderson. I knew them both well, having served under them as Junior Third Officer in the old champion trans-Atlantic liner, S.S. *Umbria*, seven years previously. Since then Captain Turner had commanded the *Caronia*, the *Carmania*, the *Mauretania* and the *Aquitania*. He had only recently taken command of the *Lucy*, relieving Captain Daniel Dow, who had commanded her in the early months of the war. He and Jock Anderson both came briefly to the port wing of the bridge to wave their greetings to former shipmates who were in the *Caronia*.

Then, through the swirling mist-veils, I saw the *Lucy*'s Second Officer, Percy Hefford. He was a special friend of mine as we had served together as First and Second Mates in an old rattletrap tramp, S.S. *Nether Holme*, before either of us had joined the Cunard service. That had been in 1906, the year the *Lusitania* was launched on the Clyde. It had been Percy Hefford's dream of ambition then to serve some day in the *Lusitania*. Now, there he was.

We semaphored to one another with our arms – 'Cheerio!' 'Good-bye!' 'Good Voyage!' 'Good Luck!'

A week later we learned the terrible news that stunned the world and, in a sense, altered the course of the war and of human history. It was the sinking of the *Lusitania* by a torpedo fired without warning by a German U-Boat – a man-made disaster more horrifying for that reason than the wreck of the *Titanic* three years previously – that aroused the intense indignation and hatred against Germany which eventually brought the U.S.A. into the war. That was the turning point in American public opinion, which, until then, had been isolationist and neutral.

The *Lusitania* disaster was immediately denounced by Britain and America as a bestial, criminal act. All newspapers in the United States took up the Allied cause and called upon President Wilson to take immediate action against Germany. The influential *Journal of Commerce* stated: 'The attack on the *Lusitania* was not war, it was simply murder on a scale deliberately intended to inspire general consternation and fear.' The New York *Tribune* declared: 'For this murder there is no justification.' A number of leading American politicians were also quick to denounce Germany's action and demand war. These included the former president, Theodore Roosevelt. But it took time for public opinion eventually to change the mind of the country's neutralist president, Woodrow Wilson, and before that happened the sinking of the *Lusitania* changed the pattern of the war at sea.

After May 1915 there were no gentlemen's agreements on the sea in the First World War. Dummy battleships were sent on patrol in the Atlantic – old cargo-steamers given false wooden hull-frames and superstructures, mounting wooden guns, and with dummy funnels and other fitments to make them look like Dreadnoughts and confuse the enemy about the dispositions of the British Fleet.

'Q' ships were used to trap submarines. These were cargo-steamers, and even sailing ships, manned by naval personnel (not in uniform), carrying concealed guns and sometimes sailing under false colours. If a U-boat ordered a 'Q' ship to stop for the inspection of its papers or cargo it would pretend to surrender, and when the submarine came nearer would suddenly reveal its guns and open fire.

Before America came into the war many British merchant ships had been known to hoist the American flag when approaching known U-boat danger areas, and revert to the British flag when reaching safer waters. In the end there were so many ruses that almost every old-fashioned rule for the honourable conduct of war at sea went by the board. But not until April 6th, 1917, did President Woodrow Wilson give in to public opinion in his country and declare war against Germany and the other powers of the Central European Alliance.

It has been generally accepted that an island nation like Britain looks 87

Please do not destroy this

When you have read it carefully through kindly pass it on to a friend.

A
German Naval Victory

"With joyful pride we contemplate this latest deed of our navy. . . ."—
Kölnische Volkszeitung, 10th May, 1915.

This medal has been struck in Germany with the object of keeping alive in German hearts the recollection of the glorious achievement of the German Navy in deliberately destroying an unarmed passenger ship, together with 1,198 non-combatants, men, women and children.

On the obverse, under the legend "No contraband" *(Keine Bannware),* there is a representation of the *Lusitania* sinking. The designer has put in guns and aeroplanes, which (as was certified by United States Government officials after inspection) the *Lusitania* did *not* carry; but has conveniently omitted to put in the women and children, which the world knows she *did* carry.

On the reverse, under the legend "Business above all" *(Geschäft über alles),* the figure of Death sits at the booking office of the Cunard Line and gives out tickets to passengers, who refuse to attend to the warning against submarines given by a German. This picture seeks apparently to propound the theory that if a murderer warns his victim of his intention, the guilt of the crime will rest with the victim, not with the murderer.

Replicas of the medal are issued by the Lusitania Souvenir Medal Committee, 32, Duke Street, Manchester Square W. 1.

All profits accruing to this Committee will be handed to St. Dunstan's Blinded Soldiers and Sailors Hostel.

The medallion was produced in Britain for propaganda purposes in order to give the impression to the United States that it was a German medal which had been struck to commemorate the sinking of the vessel as a deliberate act of war.

upon its merchant fleet to help in time of war, and in common with all British shipping companies, Cunard has played its part in the many emergencies that have occurred since its foundation. The First World War was no exception and between 1914 and 1918, Cunard vessels transported nearly one million troops and ten million tons of cargo, serving also as hospital ships, armed merchant cruisers and depot ships.

Cunard's role started in 1914 with the requisitioning of the *Aquitania*, *Caronia* and *Carmania*. *Aquitania* had only made three commercial voyages to New York before being commandeered into service as an armed merchant cruiser and troopship. She was stripped of all her luxury fittings and furniture in Merseyside, Liverpool, and all this material, in brand new condition, had to be hastily taken out and stored in warehouses ashore. Five thousand men were engaged in 'gutting' the *Aquitania* and the *Caronia*, berthed alongside her, and 2,000 wagon-loads of material were removed from the two liners within 48 hours. After first serving as an armed cruiser, *Aquitania* was engaged as a troopship. From September 1915 until Christmas 1916 she was used as a hospital ship. During 1917 she was laid up but resumed service in March 1918 as a troopship.

Caronia (I) was commissioned as an armed merchant cruiser at the start of the war and attached to the West Indies and North American stations. Later she was engaged in trooping between South and East Africa and India until returned to Cunard service.

The other half of the 'Pretty Sisters' team, *Carmania*, also fitted out as an armed cruiser, took part in one of the classic sea battles of the First World War when she fought and sank the German armed cruiser, *Cap Trafalgar*, near Trinidade Island in the South Atlantic in September 1914.

The newly launched *Cap Trafalgar*, the proud flagship of the Hamburg–Sud-Amerika Line, approximately the same size and speed as *Carmania*, had left Buenos Aires on August 15th and had been converted at sea into an armed merchant cruiser under the German war flag. Her superstructure appearance had also been disguised and her funnels repainted in red and black Cunard colours. As she headed for a rendezvous off Trinidade Island, a mid-ocean haven off the east coast of Brazil, her captain received orders to destroy all British shipping heading north from the Plate.

What happened when *Carmania* and *Cap Trafalgar* subsequently met became a case of two armed merchant liners slugging it out with their guns in the tradition of olden times, ship to ship, both becoming heavily damaged by gunfire but without ever a thought of running away.

The two former luxury liners first engaged each other with 4.7 and 4.1 inch guns respectively at 7,000 yards range on a fine September morning. Of the ensuing battle, Kenneth Poolman, the well known writer on naval affairs, gives a graphic round by round description in his book *Armed Merchant Cruisers*.

Cap Trafalgar's first round went over, *Carmania*'s fell short. *Cap Trafalgar*'s second shell brought down *Carmania*'s signal halliards and wireless mast. The third disabled one of her guns, killing the gun-layer and sight-setter and wounding all the others in the gun's crew.

Then two shells from *Carmania* shattered the Winter Garden (an elaborate aft glass superstructure on the former German liner) and knife-edged shards of glass and wood flew round the decks, killing men, severing steam pipes. But the range was closing fast and in a few minutes *Cap Trafalgar* would be able to use her three forward heavy 3.7 cm pom-pom type machine guns. Then another shell burst near the bridge. Splinters killed the quartermaster, the wheel spun and the ship yawed to port. Wirth (Kapitan Julius Wirth, commander of the *Cap Trafalgar*) and Leutnant Rettberg heaved at the wheel but with steam and hydraulic lines cut it was almost impossible to move it. A pall of smoke and hissing steam hid the *Carmania*, away to starboard. She had now brought two more guns into action.

But the crew of the German's 4.1 could see the enemy, and opened a rapid fire on her. In minutes the *Carmania*'s bridge was on fire. Then *Cap Trafalgar* slowly came back on course. The smoke was being blown to starboard, masking her guns. Wirth shouted down to the for'ard gun crew, 'Fire at the gun flashes!' A shell from *Carmania* burst on the foc'sle 10.5, jamming it solid. The crew were badly wounded and a sharp splinter decapitated the officer of the quarters.

Suddenly the wind dropped. Wirth saw the enemy clearly on his starboard bow, about a mile away. Now was the time. He ran to the bridge rail, shouted to his three starboard machine-guns to open fire, ran back to the wheel and lent his weight to try to turn the *Cap Trafalgar* toward the British AMC.

Carmania's bridge was already almost consumed with flames, and the hail of pom-pom shells stopped all fire control efforts.

Carmania swung to starboard. The north-east wind blew the raging flames over her bows. The after port guns were still firing. The *Cap Trafalgar*'s guns were also firing, hitting *Carmania*'s masts, boats, ventilators and derricks, and keeping heads down on deck. As *Carmania* continued her turn, her starboard guns came to bear. Lockyer (the First Lieutenant and Gunnery Officer, a retired R.N. Lieutenant-Commander of nearly seventy years of age) ran along the upper deck shouting, 'Individual fire! Aim for her water line!'

Grant [Captain of *Carmania*] watched the enemy turn on her heel to starboard to follow him. The range was only about 1,000 yards as it was. The shells from five of his guns hit *Cap Trafalgar*'s water line. Round after round punched through the thin plating. One burst in a bunker, another right on the junction of the boiler-room bulkhead and the side. The bulkhead collapsed and the sea poured in. Another exploded in a for'ard reserve bunker. The stokehold was flooded in seconds . . .

At 12.30 p.m. the *Cap Trafalgar* was about 5,500 yards on *Carmania*'s starboard bow, taking water fast and badly on fire below.

But Grant also had his problems. A shell from the enemy's after gun

Carmania's bridge and chart house after her fight with the armed liner *Cap Trafalgar*.

had shot away his after emergency steering controls and orders had to be passed down to the engine room and tiller flat through open hatchways. And he had no wireless, and no compass to con the ship with. Worse still, with all the water mains severed, an almost uncontrollable fire was raging below in the main dining room and some of the cabins. Grant sent Barr [acting as navigator and adviser] below with spare hands to tackle the fire, and young Midshipmen Colson and Dickens recovered the compass from the burning navigating bridge at the cost of badly burned faces and hands . . .

The *Cap Trafalgar* was listing badly to starboard now. Men were jumping into the sea, and the few boats left seaworthy were being lowered. Sharks took three of the swimmers. The *Carmania* ceased fire and turned back downwind to help keep the flames down, while her men fought the blaze with buckets of water and stokehold shovels.

On the steeply canting bridge of the *Cap Trafalgar*, Wirth was dying from a deep splinter wound in his armpit. He asked the burly Leutnant Steffan to shout for three cheers for the Kaiser. The cheering from the boats turned into singing. The *Cap Trafalgar* began slowly to right herself, then settled gently by the bow. Suddenly she lifted her stern high in the air and plunged below. It was 1.50 p.m., one hour and forty-six minutes from the firing of the first shot.

At the end, there were cheers from the victors in crippled *Carmania*

91

for the gallantry of the losers as the *Cap Trafalgar* went down with colours flying. Nine of *Carmania*'s crew, under the command of Captain Noel Grant, R.N., with Cunard's Captain James 'Foggy' Barr acting as his navigator and adviser, were killed in the action, and 26 wounded.

H.M.S. *Mauretania* arriving at New York, December 1st, 1918, with first contingent of returning American troops.

Carmania, with her dead and wounded, managed to limp back to port the next day. Captain Grant and Captain Barr were both awarded the C.B. Lieutenant-Commander Lockyer received the D.S.O. After being invalided home, Captain Barr soon returned to sea to be given command of the Cunard troopships, *Mauretania*, *Saxonia* and *Carpathia*. He retired as Senior Commodore in 1916 and died in 1937. The *Carmania* returned to Cunard service after the war and was finally broken up in 1925.

Campania was taken over by the Admiralty in 1914 and converted into a seaplane carrier. In 1918 she was sunk in the Firth of Forth after being in collision with H.M.S. *Revenge*.

* * *

Laconia became an armed cruiser on special service off the East African coast and took part in the action which led to the destruction of the German armed cruiser, *Konigsberg*, in the Rufigi River. After returning to Cunard's North Atlantic service she was sunk by a German submarine on February 25th, 1917.

Mauretania, stripped of her luxurious furnishings and fittings, was converted into a troopship in 1915, became a hospital ship in 1916, and a transport in 1917, fitted with six-inch guns. The nearest she came to disaster was in the Aegean Sea in 1915 when a U-boat, operating in the Mediterranean, launched twin torpedoes aimed to strike her broadside on. Only a sharp look-out and a brilliant piece of quick manoeuvring following orders to the helm by Captain Daniel Dow saved the giant ship. Both torpedoes were seen to pass under *Mauretania*'s stern, one missing by five feet, the second by thirty feet. The Grand Old Lady did magnificent service throughout the war and was 'dazzle-painted' in extraordinary diamond-shaped patterns of black, white and grey, in an attempt to disguise her identity and make her more difficult to sight at sea. Finally, *Mauretania* took part in the repatriation of troops in 1919.

Franconia and *Alaunia* were in service as troopships from September 1914 carrying reinforcements from Canada and voyages to India and the Mediterranean. Both ships were sunk by German submarines in 1916. *Andania*, *Ascania*, *Ivernia* and *Saxonia* were turned into prison ships and transports. Altogether during the First World War, Cunard ships carried some 900,000 troops and 10 million tons of cargo. Many more Cunard ships than mentioned here saw active service and the company made other contributions to the war effort which were not generally known at the time.

At Cunard's engine works the company fitted out seaplane carriers and other vessels for the government. A branch engine shop at Bootle, Liverpool, was converted into a shell factory employing 1,000 workers. The company's laundry was turned over to provide facilities for military hospitals. And the company further diversified by running an aircraft factory at Aintree, Liverpool.

Towards the end of 1916 the unrestricted U-boat campaign had become so intensified that an average of 100 merchant ships were being sunk every month, mostly around the western coasts of Britain and France. Apart from the two Cunarders, *Franconia* and *Alaunia*, sunk in October that year, the giant White Star *Britannic* (46,000 tons), in service as a hospital ship, sank after striking a German mine in the Aegean on November 21st, 1916.

In the first four months of 1917, 1,208 British and Allied ships were sunk, and by the end of the war in 1918, Cunard had lost a total of 22 ships by enemy action, 3 of them the Cunard liners *Andania* (13,000 tons), *Aurania* (II) (13,900 tons) and *Carpathia* (13,600 tons) in the last year of the war. Other Cunarders lost included *Ultonia* (4,750 tons); *Veria* (3,200   93 tons); *Ivernia* (I) (14,066 tons); *Lusitania* (31,550 tons); *Thracia* (2,891 tons); *Lycia* (2,715 tons); *Franconia* (I) (18,149 tons); *Caria* (3,304 tons); *Vandalia* (I) (7,333 tons); *Valeria* (burnt out) (5,865 tons); *Laconia* (I) (18,099 tons); *Ascania* (I) (wrecked) (9,111 tons); *Ausonia* (I) (7,907 tons); *Alaunia* (13,405 tons); *Volodia* (5,689 tons); *Vinovia* (5,503 tons); *Flavia* (9,291 tons); *Feltria* (5,253 tons) and *Folia* (6,704 tons).

On top of these losses, Cunard also had to take into account those suffered by the cargo ships of the Commonwealth and Dominion Line (later to become the Port Line), which they had acquired in 1916, and Thos. and Jno. Brocklebank, a long established cargo line in which Cunard had interests during the First World War and of which they finally acquired 60 per cent of shares in 1919.* The newly formed Commonwealth and Dominion Line had hardly had time to get into working order when war broke out and of the line's 25 ships afloat on August 4th, 1914, 7 were lost by enemy action, and 2 others by collision. Brocklebank's lost 9 ships during the course of the war.

---

*See following chapter (Chapter 8) and Chapter 13, for further details concerning Port Line and Brocklebanks.

CHAPTER EIGHT

A Queen is Born

Cunard emerged from the First World War in a far healthier position than many other shipping companies, as was aptly explained by a company director in 1919: 'We begin the new era of peace under very favourable auspices,' he told shareholders, 'although it is useless to disguise the fact that the national position is sufficiently serious to shake the confidence of the most optimistic.'

In that one paragraph the story of the next decade and a half was put in a nutshell as far as Cunard was concerned: it was to culminate in one of the biggest gambles, the building of the *Queen Mary* in the early 1930s, one of the biggest liners the world has known, a wonder ship created to recapture for Britain the prestige of the seas, born at a time when passenger and freight traffic was in steep decline, and the country was in the throes of one of its worst periods of economic depression.

Long before the idea of the *Queen Mary* was conceived, Cunard had been busy using all resources to make good wartime losses, and by 1925 they had taken delivery of thirteen ships including eight new passenger steamers, most of them with the names of vessels lost during the war to be used on both United States and Canadian routes. They were the *Scythia* (II), *Samaria* (II) and *Laconia* (II), all of 20,000 tons; the *Tyrrhenia* (later named *Lancastria*) (16,000 tons); and four 'A' Class ships, the *Andania* (II), *Ausonia* (II) and *Antonia*, all of 14,000 tons; and the *Albania* (13,000 tons). The 'A' Class ships were oil-fired turbines and had the capacity for carrying both passengers and cargo.

Most shipping companies were desperately building and buying vessels to cope with peacetime trading and to replace the frightful losses. Cunard, luckier than most, had come out of the war in a fairly strong financial position and still had two medium-sized passenger liners surviving, the *Saxonia* (14,280 tons) and the *Pannonia* (9,851 tons), as well as the four big speedy liners of pre-war days, the *Aquitania*, *Mauretania* (converted to an oil-burner shortly after the end of the war), *Caronia* and *Carmania*.

There were also five small cargo-steamers of pre-war vintage, averaging 3,000 tons but unsuitable for the trans-Atlantic service, and during the war Cunard had been able to buy or build some 16 single-screw cargo-steamers, averaging 5,000 tons, of which 7 had survived.

The company had grown in other ways since the turn of the century by a merger in 1912 with the Anchor Line (Henderson Bros. Ltd), which had a large cargo trade with the East; and the acquisition in 1916 of the whole of the share capital of the Commonwealth and Dominion Line (later to   95 become the Port Line), a large private company engaged in the refrigerated and general cargo trades between the United Kingdom and Australia/New Zealand, and also between the East Coast of North America and Australia/New Zealand. The merger in 1919 with the long-established cargo shipping line of Thos. and Jno. Brocklebank Limited began a long and important relationship between Cunard and members of the family of a Liverpool shipping company, Edward Bates and Sons. In 1911, Edward Bates and Sons had bought half Brocklebank's shares and from 1919 this meant Cunard's relationship with the Bates family would be close and continuous and, in fact, it was to be a powerful force in Cunard's post-war history.*

Sir Percy Elly Bates, who first joined Cunard as a non-executive director in 1912, and became chairman of the Cunard Steam-Ship Company in 1930, was responsible for negotiating the 'Big Ship' policy which led to the building of the *Queen Mary* and the *Queen Elizabeth* (I). He was also on the board of the *Morning Post*, the one-time prominent London daily newspaper founded in 1772, which amalgamated with the *Daily Telegraph* in 1937. Sir Percy was followed as Cunard chairman in 1946 by his brother, Frederick Alan Bates, who was also a guiding force during the 'Big Ships' negotiations; and he in turn was followed into the chair by a third brother, Colonel Denis Haughton Bates, who had built up Brocklebanks.

In economic terms the mergers had secured for Cunard control over a vastly increased tonnage acquired at relatively low cost compared with post-war inflated prices. The company had also been able to pay off nearly £1,300,000 of its mortgage debt to the government and by the end of 1919 it owned, or controlled through its new associate companies, an aggregate of 559,380 tons of shipping with another 426,800 tons under construction for the various companies.

To compensate for the loss of *Lusitania*, Cunard acquired the enormous German liner, *Imperator* (52,226 tons) which was re-christened the *Berengaria*. The *Imperator* had remained in harbour in Germany during the war, was taken over by the U.S.A. soon after the Armistice and taken to New York. She was handed over to Cunard after inter-Allied discussions.

As Cunard continued to build up its trade routes in both passengers and cargo, other countries were busily engaged in the 'Big Ship' building race to gain supremacy of the North Atlantic. The carriage of emigrants had become a much less important element in earning capability and new fields were being explored by both Cunard and its rivals. There were two new types of passenger to cater for – a luxury class including royalty, aristocrats of many nations, millionaires, statesmen, theatrical people, sportsmen and sportswomen, and other world celebrities, and a new tourist trade consisting of many of the two million Americans who had crossed the Atlantic in the fighting services during the war and wanted to re-trace their steps in peacetime, mainly in Britain and France.

---

*The story of the cargo and freight side of the company, including the birth of the container revolution of the 1960s, is told in Chapter 13.

Berengaria: formerly the German liner *Imperator* and acquired by Cunard in compensation for the loss of *Lusitania*.

Soon competing for this business in the 1920s was the most formidable fleet of international giant liners ever seen on the Atlantic, and these included what were then the three biggest ships in the world, the former German liner *Bismarck* (56,551 tons), which had been handed over to the White Star Line and renamed *Majestic*; the German built *Vaterland* (59,957 tons), renamed the *Leviathan*, and put into service as an American-owned passenger liner, one of six former German liners run by United States lines; and Cunard's *Berengaria*.

In 1921, the Compagnie Générale Transatlantique (French Line) launched the *Paris* (34,569 tons) and in 1927, the *Ile De France*, (43,153 tons). The Norddeutscher Lloyd Line, even after Germany's defeat, launched the *Columbus* (32,567 tons) in 1922; in 1928 the *Europa* (49,746 tons); and in 1929 the *Bremen* (51,731 tons). The Italian Line launched two big liners in 1932, the *Rex* (51,062 tons) and the *Conte Di Savoia* (48,502 tons). In 1935, the French Line put into service their superliner, *Normandie* (82,000 tons).

It was obvious that Cunard could not match the competitive strength of other lines in this new and specialized type of business with just five liners, four of them pre-war. They did their best, however, from a greatly inferior position. The *Mauretania* was soon operating from Southampton and calling at Cherbourg and managed to remain a favourite with Atlantic passengers, always having 'The Roast Beef of Old England', served from big sirloin joints at table. And the convention of dining at the captain's table in the *Aquitania*, with Commodore Sir James Charles as host, was 97 something never to be forgotten. Sir James is said to have first established the grand manner in captain's hospitality by strict protocol, and a contemporary description of dining at Sir James's table goes:

> It was an age when the dinner jacket was not in universal acceptance among Englishmen as evening attire, and one's steward, on instructions from the bridge, laid out smoking or tails as the Commodore might have decreed and left a note making the dinner hour. You didn't dine at your convenience but the Commodore's, and on evenings of the Captain's Dinner full evening dress was required with decorations, which put Americans, unless they were of military background, at a disadvantage in the matter of crosses, ribbons and miniatures.
>
> Sir James's tastes at table were vaguely those of Emil Jannings playing Henry VIII. Stewards rolled in carcasses of whole roasted oxen one night, and the next evening small herds of grilled antelope surrounded a hilltop of Strasbourg foie gras surmounted by peacock fans. Electrically illuminated pièces montées representing the Battle of Waterloo and other patriotic moments made an appearance while the ship's orchestra played Elgar. Chefs in two-foot high hats blossomed towards the end, like the final set pieces of a Paine's firework display on the Fourth of July. Throughout these flanking moments and skirmishes champagne circulated in jeroboams, Mumms 1916, Irroy, and Perrier-Jouet . . .

The Americans loved it. The English took it in their stride. But the Scots were not amused at having their prime Angus beef described as 'The Roast Beef of Old England'!

Adverse trading conditions at the start of the 1930s, worldwide depression, and the success of the initiative of foreign countries with their Atlantic 'Big Ships', meant Cunard had to do something dramatic to regain supremacy. British earnings from passenger traffic on the North Atlantic had fallen from over £9 million in 1928 to under £4 million in 1931. The only answer appeared to be in the laying down of a new ship, or two new ships, of such immense size and power that they would sustain the company's most valuable assets, prestige and goodwill. At a board meeting held in October 1929 it was decided that one ship should be built to replace the *Mauretania* (with the possibility of a sister ship to follow), and that it should be of revolutionary design and of great size, power and speed.

Sir Aubrey Brocklebank, a Cunard director, was put in charge of early specifications and design, and after 7,000 experiments with no less than 16 different models in a tank simulating every kind of weather to be expected on the Atlantic, a ship of around 1,000 feet overall, with a beam of 119 feet and a gross tonnage of 81,000, was decided upon. She was to be the 148th Cunard liner to be put into ocean-going service in 98 years, and, despite her immense bulk, her hull would need the graceful lines of a yacht if she

R.M.S. *Mauretania*: a corner of the dining saloon with oak panelling.

Aquitania: after end of smoking room.

(*Below*) Second-class *Aquitania* (lounge dancing) taken May 27th, 1928.

250 Grouse
250 Partridge
800 Quail
200 Snipe
400 Pigeons
60 Lambs
10 Calves
40 Oxen
200 Pheasants
80 Sheep
2,000 Fowls
130 Pigs
150 Turkeys
350 Ducks
90 Geese

was to set a new record across the Atlantic.

The tasks of obtaining early finance for building the ship at a time when shipping company balance sheets were being regarded with critical and suspicious interest; obtaining government backing; and conducting complicated negotiations in relation to plans for the merging of Cunard with the White Star Line – all this was placed on the shoulders of Sir Percy Bates, who had succeeded Sir Thomas Royden as chairman.

Eventually, private backers were found so that a start could be made, and in December 1930, the formal contract for the construction of Cunarder No. 534 was signed with the famous firm of Messrs John Brown of Clydebank and the laying of the great liner's keel-plates was begun. The immediate preceding years had not been good for work on Clydeside and the contract for No. 534 not only promised jobs for thousands of unemployed but became a symbol of hope for the future, and a sign that the great days of shipbuilding had not gone for good.

The skeleton of the great ship grew, rising from the river bed, first to the level of the dockyard walls, and at last to tower above the tallest buildings and become the most conspicuous landmark in all Clydeside. No. 534 was to be a ship of peace. Her purpose to carry travellers and strengthen ties of friendship between two nations, Britain and the New World of America.

The livestock, birds, etc, necessary to supply the *Lusitania* or *Mauretania* with meat, game and bacon.

(*Right*) Cunard White Star poster.

VISIT AMERICA

CUNARD WHITE STAR

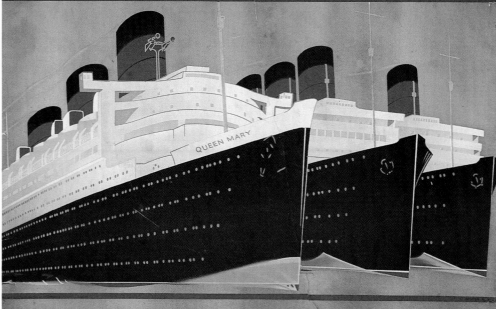

THE "QUEEN MARY"
IN ONE OF THE KITCHENS

THE "QUEEN MARY": Capt. SIR EDGAR BRITTEN
INSPECTING ONE OF THE ANCHORS

THE "QUEEN MARY":
THIRD CLASS STATEROOM

THE "QUEEN MARY": SPECIAL SUITE, MAIN DECK

THE "QUEEN MARY": VERANDAH GRILL, SUN DECK

THE "QUEEN MARY": SUN DECK

Second-class *Aquitania* taken May 27th, 1928.

(*Left*) Cigarette cards of the *Queen Mary*.

Her construction was work in which all men could take part with pride and satisfaction.

For twelve months the work went on at full speed. The girders arose from the keel-plates, 10 million rivets clamped the steel shell to the massive frame, 2,000 port-holes and windows were cut, 12 great decks had to be laid, and the enormous shafts that would turn the 4 propellers had to be transported and fixed into position.

Work was months ahead of schedule when, on December 10th, 1931, almost exactly a year after the signing of the contract, the board of Cunard wrote to shareholders notifying them that 'the directors have reluctantly decided that it is necessary to suspend the construction of No. 534 pending some change in prospect.' The company had been harder hit by the decline in passenger and cargo traffic than expected and, being dependent upon private finance, the directors felt unable to proceed with a six-million-pound supership when there was not enough custom for the old, and all

103

The *Queen Mary* under construction – work was months ahead when suddenly it was suspended and thousands were made jobless.

efforts to obtain further financial support had been met by firm refusal from banks, financial houses and the Treasury.

At first the working men of Clydeside could hardly believe the news – work on the new vessel to be abandoned halfway through, after twelve months of determined toil and the spending of £2,000,000. The decision affected directly, and at once, the 3,000 men who had been working on No. 534, and indirectly some 6,000 to 7,000 more engaged in factories and workshops on sub-contract work all over the country. Not only was it to be a black Christmas and Hogmanay on Clydeside, but for 2½ years men were to remain out of work and on the dole as No. 534 was left unfinished in the yards.

Meanwhile, Members of Parliament and newspapers throughout Britain continued to urge the government to come to the aid of Cunard so that the great liner, on which so much had already been spent, could be completed. Sir Percy Bates, a shrewd negotiator and a man of dogged resolution, supported by the no less forceful personality of his brother, Frederick, continued the fight for government support, but it became more and more evident that this would only be forthcoming if Cunard absorbed the Oceanic Steam Navigation Company, better known as the White Star Line. Cunard did not consider the White Star Line as an asset. At one stage in the negotiations, Sir Percy wrote to Lord Weir, a former Minister of Aircraft Production appointed by the government to conduct a confidential enquiry into the trading and financial position of British shipping companies engaged on the North Atlantic:

A crude statement of the situation would read something like this. H.M. Government say to Cunard, 'arrange to absorb Oceanic which as an entity we think has no chance of survival, and we will help you on No. 534 and her sister'.

This is quite sound logic and sound policy; but H.M. Government, in one form or another, is the principal creditor of Oceanic and first of all by lending her more money to lose and, later, by agreeing to a moratorium, has placed it in a negotiating position which, from the Cunard angle is impossible.

How near the truth Sir Percy had come was revealed some years later with the publication of an extract from the private diary of the then Chancellor of the Exchequer, Neville Chamberlain. This diary entry read: 'My own aim has always been to use the 534 as a lever for bringing about a merger between Cunard and White Star Lines thus establishing a strong British firm in the North Atlantic trade.' The argument was tossed from one side to the other whilst, in Parliament, efforts to secure resumption of the work on No. 534 continued unabated to be eventually put in the most forceful manner by David Kirkwood M.P. on behalf of his out-of-work constituents on Clydebank: 'I believe that as long as No. 534 lies like a skeleton in my constituency so long will the depression last in this country,' he told the House of Commons. 'To me it seems to shout, "Failure! Failure!" to the whole of Britain, and that is how others look at it.'

Finally, the government relented and decided to provide the necessary finance to enable work on No. 534 to re-start, conditional on the fusing of British shipping interests in the North Atlantic and making the Cunard and White Star companies become a single combine. A bill was immediately introduced into the House of Commons authorizing the Treasury to advance up to £9,500,000 towards the completion of No. 534, and possibly the construction of a sister ship. Three million pounds would be for the completion of No. 534, £1,500,000 as working capital, and £5,000,000 was to be made available if it were decided later on to build a sister ship.

In many ways it was another good deal for Cunard: it meant resumption of work on No. 534, some working capital, and a loan for the prospective laying down of a sister ship (*Queen Elizabeth I*). On the other hand not much was to be gained from the merger with White Star except ten ships with limited life, and a new name at Lloyd's – Cunard White Star Limited.

On April 3rd, 1934, to the skirl of bagpipes, the first 300 men marched back through the gates of John Brown's on Clydeside to scour off tons of rust from 534's hull and scare away colonies of birds who for twenty-eight months had made their homes in the steel girders. Within a few weeks thousands of men were back on the ship, most of whom had been without work and on the dole since the building was suspended in 1931. As soon as the dockyard work was resumed factories and workshops which had been engaged on contract and sub-contract work for the huge liner when work

The launching of the *Queen Mary* by Queen Mary.

was suspended called back their work forces. An estimated 10,000 men all over Britain were made busy again supplying the ship's many needs.

From the famous Belfast firm of Harland and Wolff's came the 4 cast-iron gear wheel centres, each weighing $51\frac{1}{2}$ tons. From Millwall, London, the 4 propellers, nearly 20 feet in diameter and the heaviest propellers ever made in one piece. From Staffordshire, the anchors; Sheffield, the boiler drums; Glasgow, the pumps; Darlington, the largest structural steel castings ever made; Rugby, the turbo-generators; London, the furnishing and panelling; Kidderminster, 6 miles of carpets and rugs; St Albans, the clocks; and Halifax, 10 miles of blankets. Thirteen miles of fabrics for curtains, loose covers and bedspreads were used in the ship; miles of telephone wire for the most complete telephone service ever installed in a ship; 500,000 pieces of linen; 200,000 pieces of earthenware, glass and china; and 16,000 pieces of cutlery and table-ware.

By the end of the summer of 1934 No. 534 was ready for launching. Months before the launching, newspapers and tipsters all over Britain put forward names which they claimed had been chosen for No. 534. These included 'Britannia', 'Marina', 'Princess Elizabeth' and 'Princess Margaret Rose'.

After the official christening a story spread through London shipping circles, and is still told to this day, that Cunard had wanted yet another name – 'Victoria' – and No. 534 had only become R.M.S. *Queen Mary* by a misunderstanding on the part of King George V. The 'Victoria' name, according to the story, had been chosen because it followed a Cunard tradition of giving their ships names ending in 'ia', starting with *Britannia* in 1840, and the misunderstanding occurred when a Cunard director went to Buckingham Palace to obtain royal consent.

Granted an audience by King George V (a grandson of Queen Victoria), the Cunard director addressed the king as follows: 'Your Majesty, the Cunard line is building the best, biggest, and speediest ship in the world, and requests your gracious permission to name her after the most illustrious and remarkable woman who has ever been Queen of England.'

The king thought for a moment, and then replied: 'My wife will be delighted!'

Before 200,000 spectators crowded together in pouring rain, the launch ceremony was performed by Her Majesty Queen Mary, wife of King George V, on September 26th, 1934, the first time a Queen of England had performed the launching of a merchant vessel. The ceremony was broadcast by the B.B.C., and it was also the first time Queen Mary's voice had been heard on radio. The name of the *Queen Mary* had been kept secret until the moment she slipped into the Clyde.

Before Her Majesty Queen Mary pressed the button which sent *Queen Mary* on her way, King George V paid a glowing tribute to 'the stateliest ship now in being'. It was a stirring speech:

As a sailor, I have deep pleasure in coming here to watch the launching by the Queen of this great and beautiful ship. The sea, with her tempests, will not readily be bridled: she is stronger than man; yet in recent times man has done much to make the struggle with her more equal.

It is still less than a hundred years since Samuel Cunard founded his service of small wooden paddle-steamers for the carrying of the mails across the Atlantic to America.

Those first Cunard ships were of 1,150 tons. A few people, now alive, must, in childhood have heard those ships spoken of with wonder as evidence of man's mastery over nature.

Today we come to the happy task of sending on her way the stateliest ship now in being. I thank all those, here and elsewhere, whose efforts, however conspicuous or humble, have helped to build her.

For three years her uncompleted hull has lain in silence on the stocks. We know full well what misery a silent dockyard can spread among a seaport, and with what courage that misery is endured. During those years when work upon her was suspended we grieved for what that suspension meant to thousands of our people. We rejoice that, with the help of my Government, it has been possible to lift that cloud and to complete this ship.

Now, with the hope of better trade on both sides of the Atlantic, let us look forward to her playing a great part in the revival of international commerce. It has been the nation's will that she should be completed, and today we can send her forth no longer a number on the books, but a ship with a name in the world, alive with beauty, energy and strength.

Samuel Cunard built his ships to carry the mails between the two English speaking countries. This one is built to carry the people of the two lands, in great numbers, to and fro, so that they may learn to understand each other; both are faced with similar problems and prosper and suffer together. May she in her career bear many thousands of each race to visit the other as students and to return as friends.

We send her to her element with the good will of all the nations, as a mark of our hope in the future. She has been built in fellowship among outselves; may her life among great waters spread friendship among the nations.

CHAPTER NINE

The Queen Sisters

At the first flush of fame for the *Queen Mary*, a glossy brochure entitled 'Atlantic Fairway' described the pleasures of crossing to America the Cunard way – 'The only way to cross'. The brochure proclaimed: 'Protected by luxury you sail the ancient path between continents, knowing its purple dawns and peach-red sunsets, the huge skies only found at sea, until, in good time you arrive at your landfall, refreshed and richer in company, with the light of the sea on your salt-tanned cheeks and a look of distance in your eyes.'

By the late 'thirties the flow of superlatives coming from the pens of Cunard's publicity staff had reached torrent proportions as they went to work promoting the worldwide image of the *Queen Mary* and her sister to follow, the *Queen Elizabeth*.

'Greatest', 'finest', 'most brilliant', 'dazzling', 'wonderful', 'splendid', 'smashing', 'classic', 'unrivalled', 'inimitable' – the descriptions read like pages from *Roget's Thesaurus* as Cunard made sure with unprecedented publicity that there were few in the English-speaking world who did not know the gigantic dimensions and luxurious appointments of the 'Queens of the Western Ocean'.

Mind you, the Cunard publicity department had plenty of facts and figures to work on. For instance: the *Queen Mary* weighed more than the total weight of the Spanish Armada; the crow's nest, 234 feet above the sea, was centrally heated; dogs had a promenade deck and their kennels had a lamp post; from the bridge the captain could close off any part of the ship and extinguish fires from his office; the ship was insured for the record sum of £4,800,000 at an annual premium of £60,000; printing presses turned out 12,000 menus a day, also a daily newspaper, the *Ocean Times*; lighting effects in the gold and silver white-floored ballroom were controlled by the tone and volume of the music; there were three cinemas aboard, one for each class; 30,000 electric light bulbs were fitted in the liner; all 24 lifeboats could be lowered in one minute; accommodation for passengers' pets was warmed in winter and ventilated in summer; the ship was the first to provide a church, a chapel and a synagogue for worship and prayer; all cabins were insulated to make them practically noiseless; in addition to the swimming pool there were Turkish and curative baths.

But it wasn't only the Cunard publicists who went overboard with the descriptive wonders of the Queens and the pleasures they offered the travellers of the day. Many well-known writers, journalists, and authors were equally enthusiastic in their praise. Author Laurie Lee, who took

An artist's impression of how the *Queen Mary* would appear if placed across Trafalgar Square.

first-class passage from New York to England, described the experience for a Cunard publication in the following way:

> Modern travel, to many, has become a form of transportation by capsule – a peremptory operation during which the ticketed traveller is delivered packaged with all possible speed. The result is exhaustion and often lack of identity. Only the sea seems to have escaped this impatience.

Deck golf on the *Queen Mary*.

At sea you are not anonymous. The time and pleasure are yours. Indeed an Atlantic crossing, either way – far more than a means of just getting there – can be a social event, a luxurious party, a long week-end with distinguished company.

Take the New York departure of one of the 'Queens'. It is something of a royal progress. It begins when you drive to the city docks and first see the great liner waiting, its shining structure and cliff-like hull riding high like an off-shore island. Its very size and beauty bestows structure upon you. You know this will be travel with a difference.

Elegant, romantic, almost medieval in its grace, it throws down gangways to greet your arrival. White-coated stewards, your name on their lips, receive you with dignity; and as you step aboard you are enveloped immediately by an assurance of warmth and space.

With visitors ashore, the liner pulls into the river, but it is the city not the ship that moves – seeming to withdraw itself from us like a reluctant hand in a long and lingering farewell. Out through the Narrows, with the coastline fading, we are the centre of a sun-blue world. Other vessels escort us through the long afternoon: Greek tankers, Swedish cargo-boats, coastguard cutters . . . The Narrows open, the land falls away, and at last we are alone. The liner leans forward into the wide Atlantic, and all the sea, and all the time, is ours.

We are travelling by a vessel founded on splendour and power almost without equal in the history of ships. Over 80,000 tons of curved steel and wood; 14 decks on a 1,000-foot keel; 1,200 crew; geared turbines of 158,000 horsepower; and high on the bridge, cool in

control, a vigil of veteran officers.

Blindfold race on the *Queen Mary*.

Below decks is that luxury, organisation and space, for which the 'Queens' are famous – vast public rooms running the breadth of the ship, long galleries and gilded staircases, the decorated dining rooms and spacious cabins, massed flowers growing in golden tubs; as well as shops, libraries, bars, beauty-parlours, swimming-pools, gymnasium and cinema. Behind all this, beyond the passenger's eye, is another world again, the larger world of the sailor's duty – wireless, paint-shops, lamp-trimmers, carpenters, fire-patrols, doctors; a telephone exchange as large as a town's, food stores, kitchen and bakeries; and below, in the great ship's cavernous core, the tropical heat of the engine rooms, where the oil-burning boilers generate sufficient power to light a city the size of Bristol.

The decks are as long as a village street, and one strides them with half-forgotten vigour. A day such as this is a kind of traveller's cheque which one spends for one's health and profit. There are deck chairs in the sun, soup and biscuits at eleven, iced drinks on a tray before luncheon, a book or siesta in the afternoon, tea and cakes at four o'clock.

Evening. Cocktail hour. The Captain has presented his compliments and requests the pleasure of your company in his quarters. High up, near the bridge, in a room like a headmaster's, you meet other of your fellow passengers. There are actors, writers, steel magnates and wives, professors, Italian princesses. The Captain, lean as a Scottish loch, orders his guests like a flagged flotilla, deploying their movements with an expert touch and bringing them trimly alongside each other.

The Observation Bar is also filling up – another meeting-place before dinner. Its great bow window holds a panorama of the evening – the ship's prow and the spread-out sea. In one's hand the martini trembles faintly. One feels the throb of the liner's thrust. Black ties and tuxedos, bare arms and pearls, a steady rise of conversation and laughter. Now is the moment of warmth and balance when every kind of communication seems easy – alone at sea on a common voyage,

Observation lounge and cocktail bar on the *Queen Mary*.

113

sharing the luxury of place and purpose. A tray of oranges stuck with beetroot roses offers hot canapes of bacon and liver. There are 40 choices of the best brand whiskies at something like two shillings, or twenty-nine cents a glass.

There are few things in eating so elaborately generous as dinner in a great Cunarder. The occasion is honoured by formal clothes. An orchestra accompanies the meal. One is greeted on entering by a loaded board displaying lobsters, pâtés and fruits. One's table is decorated with ice-fresh flowers and coloured menus bound with golden thread. Embedded within them is a range of dishes that almost robs one of the power of choice . . . Pressed Boar's Head, for instance, Braised Haunch of Venison, Escargots à la mode de l'Abbaye, Roast Vermont Turkey, Paella a la Valenciana, Entrecôte Steak Henri IV. A host of waiters surround one's table, adding further suggestions of their own, while the wine-steward, loaded with chains like a mayor, advises on the best of his vintages. One settles perhaps for Caviar de Beluga, Boston Sole, and a split Bordeaux pigeon, with a bottle of Chablis and a light Bordeaux wine, and brandy and figs to follow. Equally well one might have Cantaloup Melon, Scotch Smoked Salmon, Lobster Thermidor, Duckling, etc.

Enough food, it seems, for a round-the-world voyage is stored here in the ice-cold rooms: fish, poultry, trays of chops, boned steaks, lambs sewn in sail-cloth, quarters of beef, £1,000 worth of caviare, 40 different kinds of fresh vegetables . . . the sea gives an appetite to which Cunard panders, and food is one of its proudest cargoes . . .

As the night settles down, gala dancing and cabaret, when to the sultry throbbing of the saxophone the honeymoon of ocean unfolds, with champagne in buckets at a quality and price not possible anywhere on land.

Such a ship as the *Queen Mary*, described by some as symbolizing Britain's emergence from the slump, dole queues and hunger marches of the 'thirties, was bound to provoke controversy, and the first war of words started with the unveiling of the works of the artists commissioned to decorate, and lavishly ornament, the interior of the great liner. As the ship was considered to be the result of a general national effort, and the product of a national demand, the Cunard White Star Company had decided to call on some forty contemporary artists and designers, all with differing styles, instead of entrusting the work to one or a small group of experts.

The overall effect was certainly different to the one expected; some critics described it as a compromise between austerity and vulgarity, embodying the spirit of modernism, and a tawdry mish-mash of styles. In one panel, Sir Stanley Spencer depicted a sweaty group of riveters straining against a metal plate; Dame Laura Knight decorated one of the cabin class private dining rooms with a scene from the Bertram Mills Circus; Doris Zinkeisen was responsible for a 1,000-foot square painting to decorate the verandah grill, the centre of sophistication in the ship; Rebel Stanton

Main lounge of the *Queen Mary*.

produced nudes and a new method, devised by himself, of treating relief in his decorations; and when the Cunard White Star chairman, Sir Percy Bates, first set eyes on the work of Duncan Grant including nudes in a painting called 'The Flower Gatherers' and described by critics as presenting a landmark in the history of decorative art, he immediately had them replaced by mirrors, declaring, 'You can give these pictures to the blind school!'

On this latter issue, which caused uproar in the art world, Raymond Mortimer, writing in the *Listener*, declared:

For my part I think the mistake was not so much to reject the pictures as ever to commission them. A super-luxury trans-Atlantic liner depends largely on the patronage of international film stars, financiers and opera singers, and their taste is presumably reflected in the international style of decoration which you find in the palatial hotels all over the world from Palm Beach to the Lido. I cannot think that such persons would take much notice of Mr Grant's panels, and it would obviously have been unwise not to give them what they prefer.

Others described the artistic efforts in the public rooms of Britain's new maritime masterpiece as essentially Anglo-American Odeon style, much of the work having been overseen by Benjamin Morris, the architect of the Cunard building in New York.

1936, the year of the *Queen Mary*'s maiden voyage, the weather in the Atlantic went down in meteorological records as among the worst in living memory, and violent storms, influenced by the Gulf Stream meeting the ice drifts from the north, found out the new *Queen*'s weakest point – a tendency to roll and vibrate at the stern when the sea was at its worst. So badly did the *Queen Mary* roll that on one occasion she went over at an angle of 44°, unsecured furniture ran amok, thousands of pieces of crockery were smashed, and there were so many accidents to passengers that a fleet of ambulances, discreetly tucked away, awaited the liner when she reached the Cunard White Star pier at the western end of 49th Street in New York.

Luckily, the menace of the sea referred to by King George V at the launching was not at its worst for the maiden voyage to New York via Cherbourg in May 1936 when stars like Frances Day, Larry Adler and Henry Hall and his British Broadcasting Corporation Dance Band (former-ly the resident dance band at the Gleneagles Hotel, Scotland) entertained the 1,849 passengers. The tendency of the liner to roll did, however, cause poor Frances Day to hold onto a piano for support when she sang 'Somewhere at Sea', the signature tune Henry Hall had written specially for the *Queen Mary*, whilst members of the band did their best to fight back sea-sickness and at the same time link up with the broadcasting hours of far-away radio stations taking programmes direct from the liner. The BBC was also up against difficulties brought on by unkindly Atlantic seas in trying to maintain an almost running commentary from a studio on board connected to twenty-eight microphone points around the ship.

The maiden voyage ended with the *Queen Mary* being given a fabulous reception at New York which included an escort of hundreds of small ships, aeroplanes, water spouts, blaring sirens, and ticker tapes and streamers in the streets.

It had never been anticipated that the *Queen Mary* would roll and consequently very little of the furniture in the passenger accommodation had been rigidly anchored to the deck. 'Teething trouble' was an early official explanation for the ship's performance during its Atlantic storms baptismal, but many of the experienced crew believed the problem was deeper rooted and that, despite all the experiments before and during the building of the *Queen Mary*, the ship was showing symptoms of being 'bottom heavy'.

There are not many of the hand-picked officers and crew of the *Queen*

Mary alive today who can recall first-hand experiences of her early days. But two men who sailed on the ship's maiden voyage, C.W.R. (Ron) Winter, a junior electrical officer, and Bill Tanner, a quartermaster, both in their seventies as this book was being written, and living within a few miles of each other on the Isle of Wight, well remember both the behaviour of the sea and the ship during the Queen Mary's early days.

Ron Winter, author of the book, *Queen Mary – Her Early Years Recalled*, talked about those unforgettable memories. At the height of one storm he saw heavily built settees, which took several men to lift, and easy chairs and tables, rolling over and over from side to side in the cabin class lounge, crashing into the bulkheads at each roll.

'The crew made valiant attempts to lash some of this furniture to the pillars in the room, but this was only partially successful, and for a couple of days and nights the furniture had to be left to its own devices as it was too dangerous to go into the room,' he explained. 'In one Tourist lounge there was a Challen upright piano and although this was latched to the bulkhead the screws ultimately pulled out and the piano came free. The result was unbelievable in the panelled room. As the piano cannoned its way around, it destroyed everything in its path, the panelling was ripped to pieces and the wooden case of the piano gradually disintegrated. After two or three days of this the piano was reduced to its iron frame plus strings, and as it cartwheeled round the devastated room it uttered the most weird cacophony of noises.

'The plight of the passengers was even worse. Alleyways from cabins to staircases were smoothly panelled in wood, and there were no handrails, nor anything to hold on to. Once you left your cabin you ricocheted from side to side with no chance of stopping yourself. Many elderly people came to grief this way.'

Within months of the maiden voyage the *Queen Mary* was withdrawn from service for an overhaul which included the stripping down of the great lounge, smoking room, a number of the luxurious state rooms, and the start of an investigation to try and discover the cause and cure for the great liner's propensity to roll. Eventually it was discovered that the *Queen Mary was* bottom heavy because her massive twenty-four boilers and engines were so low down in a high superstructure hull. It took a year, and a comprehensive reconstruction which included placing an additional weight of steel and water ballast high up in the ship, before the problem was rectified.

Quartermaster Bill Tanner took his turn at the wheel of the *Queen Mary* not only on her maiden voyage, but also on some thirty following voyages up to the outbreak of the Second World War. He now lives in the pretty little yachting village of Seaview on the Isle of Wight with views from his cottage of Spithead, the scene of many great moments in Britain's maritime history. He described the two brass steering wheels of the *Queen Mary* as being strangely small and toy-like compared with the massive wooden spoked wheels of Samuel Cunard's days. Only 24 inches in diameter, they operated two entirely different sets of telemotor steering

(*Left*) Cunard bell boys. Many went home with pockets stuffed with pound notes and dollars from tips.

(*Right*) Cunard White Star sailings to U.S.A.

gear, one for emergency use.

'You could turn those little wheels with a finger,' said Bill. 'What a difference to the old days.'

To starboard of the steering wheels there was a new automatic pilot known as 'Iron Mike', one of the first auto-pilots fitted in a liner and not entirely trusted by captains or quartermasters.

'You could go ten to fifteen degrees off course when the *Queen Mary* yawed,' Bill added. 'And did she yaw with a following sea! On those occasions the man at the wheel would anticipate "Iron Mike" and beat it to a new course. All the captains preferred having a man at the wheel

CUNARD WHITE STAR

U.S.A. · CANADA

QUEEN MARY	Apr.	15
° ASCANIA · · ·	–	21
AQUITANIA · ·	–	22
° AUSONIA · · ·	–	28
QUEEN MARY	May	3
GEORGIC · · ·	–	4
° ALAUNIA · · ·	–	5
AQUITANIA · ·	–	10
° AURANIA · · ·	–	12
QUEEN MARY	–	17
BRITANNIC ·	–	17
° ASCANIA · · ·	–	19

—— NEW YORK DIRECT
○ QUEBEC & MONTREAL

(*Left*) Cabin class children's playroom on *Mauretania* (II).

(*Left, below*) An impression of the Restaurant, C Deck, of the *Queen Mary*, by H. Davis Richter, R.I., R.O.I., showing the position of Philip Connard's painting and the double bronze doors by Walter and Donald Gilbert.

rather than rely on the automatic. And coming into port "Iron Mike" was never used. That was always left to human judgment.'

Bill Tanner faced most of the Atlantic hazards during his three years in the *Queen Mary*.

'You were never really lucky enough to get five good consecutive days of weather on an Atlantic run,' he said. 'And we often encountered icebergs on the northern route. I used my nose to detect them. We could smell icebergs when we were getting too close to them. The first warning you got was a tingling in your nose!'

Wages in the British Merchant Service were not generally considered good in the 1930s. Cunard, however, was known as one of the better payers, and, by so doing, employed the best crews.

'By the time I joined the *Queen Mary* as a quartermaster conditions were not bad at all,' Bill explained. 'We had good money for the day, saved it whilst at sea, and spent it when we came home. And the food aboard was good. We slept six to a cabin and each of us was provided with a reading lamp and curtains.

'Some of the crew, of course, did much better. I knew bedroom and promenade deck stewards who became rich men with tips from affluent passengers. Some stewards on the *Queen Mary* were making as much money as the captain. I will never forget one day, just before the *Queen Mary* was about to leave Southampton, our captain leaned over the wing of the bridge and spotted a bedroom steward arriving in his car to join the ship. "Just look at that," the captain called out to us. "A steward driving a Daimler and I have to put up with a Morris!" '

Bill Tanner's first captain on the *Queen Mary* was Sir Edgar Britten, a Yorkshireman educated at King Edward's School, Birmingham. It was not an uncommon sight, when arriving back at Southampton, to see Sir Edgar walking down the gangway with a parcel of washing under his arm, passing a line of cars on the dockside occupied by wives of stewards waiting for their husbands while he was on the way to catch a tram. Even bell-boys were known to go home after a voyage with pockets stuffed with pound notes and dollars from tips.

The cost to the passenger for being cosseted in the lap of luxury (weather permitting) on an Atlantic run in the *Queen Mary* in the 'thirties? It was: Cabin Class – £53.15s (£102 return); Tourist – £28.10s single (£52.10s return); Third Class – £18.10s (£33.10s return). These fares were slightly increased during August and September.

You could get a bottle of champagne for £1 and bottles of the best wines from between 10s and 4s 6d. Ladies could have a permanent wave in the hairdressers for £2.50s and men could have a hair cut for 2s and be shaved for a shilling. Whisky and gin was 10d a glass, beers 6d per bottle, and cigarettes 10d for twenty. The *Queen Mary*'s verandah grill barman was one of the busiest men on the ship and after the maiden voyage was able to bank a sum of over £200. All from tips!

Once over her initial faults, the *Queen Mary* never looked back. She became a favourite with crew and passengers and her sixteen turbines and quadruple screws helped her make the Atlantic crossing in record time.

Although Atlantic liners had competed with each other for the fastest crossings from the early days of the first Cunard steamships, the Blue Riband Trophy itself, a four-foot tall gold and silver award, did not come into being until 1935, when it was donated by Mr Harold Hales, a British businessman and a Member of Parliament.

The *Queen Mary* took the trophy from the French Line's *Normandie* on her sixth voyage in August 1936, making the westbound crossing in 4 days, 27 minutes, at a speed of over 30 knots. In 1937 the *Normandie* struck back, getting the crossing time down to 3 days, 22 hours, and 7 minutes, at a speed of over 31 knots, only to be beaten again by the *Queen Mary* the following year with a time of 3 days, 20 hours, and 40 minutes (31.69 knots). This record stood until 1952 when the *Queen Mary* was finally overtaken by the liner *United States* whose crossing that year remains the record.

The trophy, now worth £75,000 for its gold and silver content alone, is kept in the U.S. Merchant Maritime Museum at King's Point, Long Island, New York.

Pop tycoon, Richard Branson, had hoped to regain the trophy for Britain when his power boat, *Virgin Atlantic Challenger*, accomplished the crossing in July 1986 in 3 days, 8 hours and 31 minutes, 129 minutes better than the record set by the liner *United States*. But experts were adamant that the *Virgin Atlantic Challenger* did not qualify for the trophy under Hales Trophy Rules, and the Curator of the U.S. Merchant Maritime Museum, Mr Frank Braynard, commented: 'Most people would agree that it was intended for the great liners and not for little toy boats that are even smaller than the lifeboats on the liners.'

The building of giant-sized liners caused a serious re-think over the question of the provision of suitable port facilities for such large vessels, and as far back as 1919 Cunard had switched the *Mauretania*, *Aquitania* and *Berengaria* from Liverpool to Southampton to maintain a weekly Atlantic service via Cherbourg. To many people, as the size of the liners increased, it appeared inevitable that Liverpool would eventually cease to be the terminal port for big new Cunarders, a prospect viewed with much misgivings by Liverpudlians who had inaugurated and thrived on the trans-Atlantic steamship traffic for nearly a century. The fact remained: the Mersey was not big enough; Southampton was nearer London by rail and much more convenient for a call at Cherbourg to serve American passengers going to and from the Continent.

So the building of the *Queen Mary* was accompanied by the construction of the King George V drydock at Southampton, the lengthening of passenger quays at Cherbourg, and the construction at New York of three 1,200-foot piers. And following the Second World War the famous Ocean Terminal came into being at Southampton on July 31st, 1950.

The *Queen Mary* was never intended as a one-off ship, and her running mate and consort, *Queen Elizabeth*, laid down at John Brown's,

The launching of the *Queen Elizabeth* in September 1938.

Clydebank, in 1936, was launched by Queen Elizabeth, wife of King George VI, in September 1938, at the time when Premier Neville Chamberlain was flying to Munich with his umbrella to see Hitler in an attempt to avert the Second World War, and the London *Daily Express* came out with its famous gaffe of a front-page headline, 'PEACE IN OUR TIME'! A year later, on the outbreak of hostilities, the *Queen Elizabeth* was still being fitted out.

Had it not been for the war, Cunard had intended taking advantage of the two great sister ships to establish a twin-shuttle weekly service across the Atlantic as a replacement for three old liners. This, however, had to wait until after the war. Early faults in the *Queen Mary* were not repeated in the *Queen Elizabeth* and she was a magnificent liner, not too different from the *Queen Mary* to the layman's eye, but considerably changed from the marine architect's viewpoint. A well deck fitted forward in the *Queen*   *123*

Mary was eliminated; only 12 boilers were needed in the *Elizabeth* compared with 24 in the *Queen Mary*; and the most obvious external difference was that the *Elizabeth* had only two funnels against the *Mary's* three. As a result, the *Elizabeth* was able to take over 200 more passengers than the *Mary* and hold more cargo. She also had a longer, sleeker look than her elder sister. Later both the *Queen Mary* and the *Queen Elizabeth* were fitted with stabilizers.

One man who was captain of the *Queen Mary* and later the last captain of the *Queen Elizabeth*, Commodore Geoffrey Marr, D.S.C., asked which of the two ships he preferred, replied that the *Queen Mary* had an air of graciousness that will never be seen again and had a wonderful reputation for being a happy ship with an intensely loyal crew; while the *Queen Elizabeth* had many features that were an improvement on her sister, and with cleaner lines was a more perfect model.

Apart from their elegance, the great sisters had gallant and meritorious roles to play in helping Britain and her Allies defeat Adolf Hitler's Nazi Germany.

Mauretania (II) at the Princes Landing Stage, Liverpool, before her maiden voyage to New York.

124

CHAPTER TEN

The Second World War: 'Another Kind of Storm'

The strength of Cunard ships and men, led by the formidable sisters, *Queen Mary* and *Queen Elizabeth*, played a major part in shortening the horror of the Second World War. In a remarkable tribute to the exceptional contribution to victory by the two *Queens*, Sir Winston Churchill sent the following message to Cunard White Star when peace returned:

> Built for the arts of peace and to link the Old World with the New, the *Queens* challenged the fury of Hitlerism in the Battle of the Atlantic. At a speed never before realised in war, they carried over a million men to defend the liberties of civilisation. Often whole divisions at a time were moved by each ship. Vital decisions depended upon their ability continuously to elude the enemy, and without their aid the day of final victory must unquestionably have been postponed. To the men who contributed to the success of our operations in the years of peril, and to those who brought these two great ships into existence, the world owes a debt that will not be easy to measure.

Cunard chairman, Sir Percy Bates, went even further in declaring that the achievement of the *Queens* shortened hostilities in Europe by a whole year.

Cunard's ships carried 9,223,181 tons of vitally needed cargo during the war years, and up to May 1945, a total of 2,223,040 troops, of which 1,243,538 were carried in *Queen Mary* and *Queen Elizabeth*. Of the eighteen passenger ships owned by Cunard White Star Limited which went to war, the company only had nine left in service by May 1945. As Sir James Bisset, a wartime captain of both the *Queen Mary* and *Queen Elizabeth*, summed it all up after it was over: 'War was, to us, the Merchant Navy, another kind of storm!'

Together, the two *Queens* became so efficient, and such a well organized team co-ordinated by the Ministry of War Transport, the War Office, the Admiralty, and U.S. Authorities on the one hand, and the ships' companies on the other, that they could each carry 15,000 troops at a time across the Atlantic, feed and house them during the voyage, disembark them, and within the space of a few days recommence the operation.

Such was their potential threat to the enemy that the German naval command offered the highest honours, and substantial financial rewards, to any U-boat captains and crews who could sink or disable either or both of the two liners. In fact, they became the most prestigious targets Hitler's

The *Queen Mary*, her
foredecks crowded with
troops on the way to war.

navy could aim for, and at the outbreak of war there were plenty of
competitors for the prize as Germany already had 200 submarines in
commission. Later, Hitler went as far as to offer the equivalent of £100,000
to any ship or submarine that could sink one of the *Queens*. But whilst a
total of 3,180 British merchant vessels were sunk between 1939 and the
end of the war with the loss of some 35,000 men of the British Merchant
Navy, the two *Queens* sailed through practically unscathed. Mainly
because of their speed, the Germans could never get near enough to them.

One tragic accident during the war marred the wonderful record of the
two sisters. On October 2nd, 1942, the *Queen Mary*, nearing home from
America with 10,000 G.I.s aboard, collided with one of her Royal Navy
escorts, the 4,200-ton cruiser, H.M.S. *Curacoa*, off the north-west coast of
Ireland and not far from Bloody Foreland and Aran Island.

The *Queen Mary* had been zig-zagging astern of the *Curacoa* and
keeping to a pattern worked out in advance by the Admiralty in London. It
was done with the aid of a klaxon above the helmsman's head, which went
off every few minutes. All the helmsman had to do when the klaxon
sounded was to alter course hard to port, or hard to starboard, and hold her
steady until the klaxon went off again.

Horrified troops on the deck of the *Queen Mary* – raw recruits from
Iowa, Chicago and the Bronx, Texans and Georgians – saw the gap
between the two narrow dangerously as the *Queen Mary* was swinging
back and forth across the wake of the cruiser escort.

126   Suddenly, within seconds, the cruiser appeared only a matter of a few

(*Top*) The *Queen Mary* cuts through her escort H.M.S. *Curacoa* in 1942 off the Irish Coast (war artist's impression).

(*Above*) The bows of the *Queen Mary* after cutting through the cruiser, H.M.S. *Curacoa*.

hundred yards in front of the liner's bows, thrusting on at 28 knots. There was a dreadful impact as the *Queen Mary*'s bows struck *Curacoa* amidships, broadside on. The immense speed and weight of the *Queen Mary* and the shape of her specially strengthened bows, shaped almost to a knife-edge at the stem, tore through the three-inch armour-plated sides of the cruiser, slicing her clean in half. Despite the initial impact, the collision sent only a tremor through the great liner, but the horrified G.I.s who had a grandstand view of the tragedy from the decks, saw it all in ghastly detail – the two halves of the cruiser rolling over and over along each side of the giant liner, then the bows of the forward half pointing straight up to the sky with black smoke pouring from her two funnels, and the stern half capsized with the twin propellers still turning uselessly in the air, then everything disappearing into the turbulence of the *Queen Mary*'s wake.

As she was forbidden to stop, the *Queen Mary* could take little part in rescue attempts. All she could do was to throw over rafts and lifejackets as she continued on her zig-zag course, leaving escorting destroyers to pick up survivors.

Of the cruiser's complement of 410, only 72 survived. The *Queen Mary* suffered damage to her stem at the water line but managed to reach the Clyde safely where she had immediate emergency repairs to the damage 127 and return across the Atlantic to Boston for dry-docking.

The sinking of H.M.S. *Curacoa* with the loss of 338 men, one of the better kept secrets of the war, was not made public until 1945 when the Lords of the Admiralty published a list of ships lost during the course of hostilities on the North Atlantic. A prolonged legal post mortem then followed to find out which of the two ships was to blame for the accident. It started with a lengthy action in the Admiralty Court in June 1945 brought by the Admiralty against Cunard White Star Limited, alleging negligent navigation on *Queen Mary*'s part; in defence, Cunard brought a counter-claim of negligence against *Curacoa*'s captain, Captain John Boutwood, D.S.O. During the hearing Trinity House Masters sat as advisers to Mr Justice Pilcher and scale-model tests were staged for members of the court in watertanks at the National Physical Laboratory at Teddington, Middlesex.

Some twenty months later, in January 1947, judgment was given. The Admiralty's case was dismissed with costs and the *Queen Mary* was found free from blame. But it did not stop there. The Admiralty took the petition to the Appeal Court and on July 30th, 1947, the appeal was allowed, the Appeal Court attributing two-thirds of the blame to H.M.S. *Curacoa*, and one-third to the *Queen Mary*. Leave to appeal to the House of Lords was then given and in February 1949, the Lords of Appeal affirmed the decision of the Court of Appeal and ordered each side to pay its own costs.

Many of the Cunard White Star ships requisitioned by the government as auxiliary armed cruisers and troop transports played as great a part in the Second World War as their forerunners in the 1914–18 war, and often took on the superior forces of the enemy, ill equipped not only in armament and armour but also in the experience of their crews. Ten days before war was declared on September 3rd, 1939, Cunard White Star had been informed that the government proposed to requisition *Ascania*, *Aurania* (II) (later to become H.M.S. *Artifex*) and *Alaunia* (II) (later H.M.S. *Alaunia*).

This was followed by further government directives and when war was declared *Scythia*, *Britannic* and *Laconia* (II) (the 19,695 ton sister ship to the liners, *Samaria* and *Scythia*) were also requisitioned. The *Scythia* was sunk in the South Atlantic in September 1942 by a German submarine which was unaware that the liner was carrying 1,800 Italian prisoners of war, many of whom perished.

On September 12th, 1942, 700 miles off Freetown in the South Atlantic, *Laconia* was hit by two torpedoes from the German submarine U-156 under the command of Commander Werner Hartenstein. As *Laconia* was sinking, the U-Boat captain, discovering the ship had been carrying Italian prisoners of war, broadcast a message to all ships in the area requesting them to assist survivors and promised not to attack any that responded.

Staying with the survivors, and with the help of two other German submarines, he collected the *Laconia*'s lifeboats into a group to await help from the Vichy French in Dakar. Four days later, however, an American

Liberator aircraft bombed the red cross marked U-156 forcing Hartenstein to jettison over 200 survivors. As a result of this attack Vice Admiral Doenitz, who became commander-in-chief of the German Navy in 1943. issued an order that in future German U-boats should not help survivors and this became known during the Second World War as 'The Laconia Order'.

Also placed under Admiralty orders were the *Carinthia* (another beautiful Cunard liner built in 1925 which made a world cruise in 1933 and was sunk by a U-boat off Ireland in June 1940); *Andania* (sunk by a U-boat off Iceland in 1940); and *Ausonia* which was sold to the Admiralty to become a heavy repair ship. *Franconia* was taken over on September 20th, 1939, and *Aquitania* on November 21st, while the *Queen Mary* was laid up in New York to be later joined by *Mauretania* (II), which had been launched in 1938 and had only completed four voyages when war broke out.

Within two months of the outbreak of the war Britain had established a Ministry of Shipping with an advisory council of well known ship owners, representatives of officers' associations and trade union leaders to give guidance on problems arising from all sections of the shipping industry. Sir Percy Bates and Lord Essendon, the former chairman of White Star, were among those invited to serve. Sir Percy also served as a member of a liner organization committee formed to assist the Ministry of Shipping in dealing with prospective programmes of supplies, particularly vital imports, to be carried by the regular shipping lines.

Early in 1940, *Aquitania*, the oldest ship in Cunard's fleet of liners, sailed for Wellington, New Zealand, and served in Australian and Indian waters until the end of 1942. *Mauretania* sailed from New York to Sydney in March 1940 where her fitting out for troop transporting was completed. Two months later she sailed from Sydney to the Clyde with 2,000 Australian troops. She then carried on troop-carrying operations between Australia, India and Africa, and was of great assistance with both troops and supplies during the critical years of the African campaign.

Britannic's wartime duties took her all over the world and on several occasions she was the Commodore ship of convoys. *Scythia* served throughout 1940–42 carrying troops to the Middle East via Cape Town. During the allied invasion of North Africa she was struck by an aerial torpedo at Algiers and had to remain there for several weeks acting as a Royal Naval barracks. *Samaria*, *Antonia* (which later became H.M.S. *Wayland*) and *Georgic* were all requisitioned in 1940. *Georgic* took part in the evacuation of Norway and was at St Nazaire at the time of Dunkirk when the *Lancastria*, taking aboard thousands of members of the British Expeditionary Force retreating from France under the German onslaught, was sunk in a concentrated attack by Junker and Dornier dive-bombers in what Churchill described as 'the most terrible disaster in our naval history'.

Lancastria, built for Anchor Line but taken over by Cunard while still on the stocks in 1922, became a favourite cruise liner of the 'thirties, sailing   *129* out of Liverpool and taking many north country people on 13-day luxury cruises to the Mediterranean for 13 guineas per person, and on 52-day cruises to South America and the West Indies for 100 guineas. On the afternoon of June 17th, 1940, *Lancastria*, having embarked some 4,000 troops and escaping civilians and lying at anchor some three miles off St Nazaire, was awaiting orders when the dive-bombers attacked. Struck by three bombs, one down a funnel, *Lancastria* sank with the loss of over 2,000 men – the heaviest death toll in any ship sunk during the war. Survivors were hampered by large quantities of bunker fuel on the sea surface caused when the ship's deep fuel-tanks were burst open by the bombs, and continuing German aerial attacks. But an estimated 2,477 men were eventually rescued, including the *Lancastria's* Master, Captain Rudolph Sharp, who had been four hours in the water when picked up. Captain Sharp was later to lose his life when *Laconia* was sunk.

News of the sinking of the *Lancastria* was not officially released in Britain until five weeks later. After the war a *Lancastria* survivors' association was formed and wreaths were laid at the annual Armistice Day parade at London's Cenotaph. In 1963 a window to the memory of the dead was unveiled at the Church of St Catherine Cree, in Leadenhall Street, London, by Admiral of the Fleet, Lord Fraser of North Cape.

To an island such as Britain, partially reliant on imports for survival, an efficient merchant cargo fleet is essential in time of war, and ships of the Port Line, and Thos. & Jno. Brocklebank fleets, the two cargo lines acquired by Cunard during the First World War, proved this point during the Second World War. The cost was high. Port Line lost 13 ships; 167 members of Port Line's sea staff, including 5 masters and 5 chief engineers, perished at sea; and 219 were taken prisoners of war.

Two of the Port Line ships, *Port Victor* and *Port Vindex*, were requisitioned when being built in 1943 and completed as the aircraft carriers, H.M.S. *Nairana* and H.M.S. *Vindex*; as such they served with the Royal Navy until the end of the war.

Brocklebanks lost 16 ships during the war, a total of 125,075 tons of shipping, and only 10 vessels survived of the pre-war fleet.

Of all the exploits of the ships of the Port Line fleet during the Second World War those of the motor ship *Port Chalmers* (8,719 tons), during two memorable and historic convoys to the George Cross island of Malta, were the most outstanding. So outstanding, in fact, that the bravery of the crew in face of the enemy was marked by the award of 25 decorations, including a D.S.O. for Captain H.G.B. Pinkney, and an O.B.E. for Captain W.G. Higgs. This was the highest number of awards given during the war to the officers and crew of any one ship under the Red Ensign (flag of the Merchant Navy).

In the first convoy of July 1941, the *Port Chalmers*, with Captain Higgs as Commodore, was carrying a cargo which included 2,000 tons of aviation spirit, food, ammunition, motor vehicles and aircraft parts, all badly needed on the island. Four cruisers and 10 destroyers escorted the convoy to Gibraltar, where they were reinforced by the aircraft carrier, *Ark Royal*, a fifth cruiser, and 6 more destroyers. After leaving Gibraltar, the fleet was heavily attacked from the air and one destroyer was hit and sunk. One of the cruisers was also severely damaged and ordered back to Gibraltar, and a near miss by a bomb disabled another destroyer which had to be towed for two days. One merchant ship was torpedoed but managed to reach her destination.

Having safely delivered her precious cargo to Malta, the *Port Chalmers* left unescorted and on the first night out was attacked by an Italian E-boat. By constant manoeuvring, and the skilful use of the 4-inch gun, which drove off the Italian each time he tried to close, the attack was frustrated. The following day, while flying the French colours as a *ruse de guerre*, *Port Chalmers* was closely followed by enemy planes. In addition to the false French colours, four scuttling charges had been placed on board to be used if capture became inevitable. To try and avoid further detection the ship took a course close to the North African coast and one night she was required to steam at full speed, in complete darkness, until breakers on the shore were spotted, when she would swiftly alter course to avoid going aground. Luckily she managed to evade the enemy and returned safely to port.

By the summer of 1942 the position of the island fortress of Malta had become desperate. To bring her urgently needed supplies of fuel and to save her people from starvation and possible surrender, a great convoy, known as 'Operation Pedestal', sailed from Britain. Fourteen of the finest and fastest British cargo liners including *Port Chalmers*, this time in the command of Captain Pinkney, were escorted by one of the most powerful naval forces in history. These consisted of the battleships *Nelson* and *Rodney*, the aircraft carriers *Victorious*, *Furious*, *Eagle* and *Indomitable*, and a large number of cruisers and destroyers.

In the Mediterranean the convoy came under constant and ferocious air and surface attack, suffering grievous losses of ships and men. The aircraft carrier *Eagle* was torpedoed and sunk on the afternoon of August 11th. On the following day the Blue Funnel Line ship *Deucalion* was hit and subsequently sunk. During the night of August 12th/13th when the convoy was off Cape Bon, H.M.S. *Manchester* was hit and sank later. H.M.S. *Cairo* and a destroyer were also torpedoed and had to be sunk later by British forces. Two merchant ships were destroyed. The *Brisbane Star*, the *Rochester Castle* and the tanker *Ohio* were all torpedoed but not put out of action.

At daybreak on August 13th the enemy's vicious attacks were resumed and several more ships were destroyed. A stick of bombs was dropped on *Waimarama* which blew up and disappeared in a few minutes. The *Ohio* was torpedoed a second time, but struggled on with her precious cargo and eventually limped into the Grand Harbour at Valetta, supported by H.M.S. *Penn* and H.M.S. *Bramham*. The *Ohio*'s master Captain Mason was later awarded the George Cross.

Through all this, *Port Chalmers* continued unharmed, fighting back all   *131*

(*Left*) Troops cheer the *Port Chalmers* as she enters the Grand Harbour at Valetta at the end of her second heroic wartime voyage to Malta in August 1942.

(*Above*) *Port Chalmers* had a charmed life. At one stage of a Malta convoy she 'caught' a German torpedo in her paravane wire.

the time with her own armaments. She had one breath-taking moment, however, as her starboard paravane (a submerged float towed from the bow of a ship to stream out at an angle and protect a ship's sides from mines) was observed to be acting strangely. When it was wound in the crew found an unexploded 21-inch torpedo entangled in the paravane by its propeller. *Port Chalmers* was stopped and the engines put astern. When the paravane was as far away as the wire permitted, it was cut adrift. Down went the paravane and torpedo, deep down into the Mediterranean where it exploded, giving the ship a tremendous shaking. Of the original convoy that left Britain, only five merchantmen eventually reached Malta, the *Port Chalmers* being the only one to do so without casualties and unharmed.

Port Chalmers saw service until the end of the war and for twenty years afterwards. During the ship's last visit to London in 1965 a special luncheon was held aboard to commemorate her part in the Malta convoys. Malta's High Commissioner, the Honourable J.F. Axisa, told guests, who included a number of the crew who took part in the historic events:

'When this gallant ship appeared at the entrance to the Grand Harbour of Valetta on that fateful August day, the people of Malta, and my Prime Minister and I were among them, lined the bastions in total disregard of the bomb hell that rained down from enemy aircraft. The greetings and cheering to the ship, to its valiant crew, and to the escorting navy, rose above the din of the anti-aircraft guns and the roar of the bombers. It was the most emotional and unforgettable scene one could witness.

'The ship's distinguished career, and the part she played in serving

Malta, will always be remembered. Her name has made history and she will live for ever.'

What of the vital roles played by the *Queens* in the Second World War? On the Sunday morning when Premier Neville Chamberlain broadcast to the British nation that war had been declared, the *Queen Mary*, carrying a record 2,332 passengers, mostly Americans returning to their homeland, was only a few hours out of New York. Once there, she waited until her wartime future could be decided.

The *Queen Elizabeth* was still in the fitting-out basin at Brown's Yard, Clydebank, when war was declared and there she remained. Then, one day at the end of February 1940, when the war was only five months' old, she did a disappearing act. One moment the world's biggest ship was sticking out like a sore thumb in the Clyde, a sitting target for the Luftwaffe; the next, painted a dull battleship grey all over, she had vanished like a ghost in the night. Where had she gone?

Placed under the command of Captain J.C. Townley, with a crew of 500 signed on for a coastal voyage, the word was put around that she was bound for Southampton for final fitting-out in the big dock. If there were any German spies in the Clyde area, and there is no doubt they were there, there was plenty of opportunity for them to discover that the *Queen Elizabeth* was bound for Southampton, for there was even a Southampton pilot aboard; harbour officials at Southampton had been given a docking plan, concocted in advance by Cunard; and packing cases containing some of the *Queen Elizabeth*'s finishing fittings had arrived in advance at Southampton docks.

On the day she was expected at Southampton the skies over the Solent were filled with Luftwaffe bombers. But the great new liner was hidden away in Scottish waters off Gourock where her crew was informed that she was not going to Southampton but on an ocean voyage. This would require the crew to sign new articles and anyone wishing not to do so was told they would be put ashore. Only a few asked to be released and those who stayed aboard were given £30 on top of their wages as 'inconvenience money'! Those who did not fancy a trans-Atlantic trip were put on a tender and sailed into the middle of the Gaerloch to wait there until the liner was well on her way to New York. On March 2nd the *Queen Elizabeth* put to sea, steamed down the Firth of Clyde, rounded the Mull of Kintyre, and, untried at sea, headed out into the Western Ocean. It was the most unusual maiden voyage of any liner.

Speed and secrecy were all the defence she had as she steamed as fast as she could for the next three thousand miles, zig-zagging furiously. Five days later she reached the Hudson River and berthed alongside the *Queen Mary* at Pier 90 in the shadow of Manhattan, the Cunard Company pier in New York. The two great sisters were together for the first time, safe in a neutral port, and America applauded the brave secret voyage. The *New York Times* declared: 'Many sagas of the sea have begun and ended in our harbour, but can old-timers remember anything to compare with the *133*

unheralded arrival of the biggest and fastest liner in the world after the most daring of all maiden crossings? The interest of New Yorkers was echoed by the admiration of Americans everywhere for those who built her, sailed her, and sent her on her way.'

Two weeks after being joined by the *Queen Elizabeth* in New York, the *Queen Mary* started her wartime career sailing for Australia, via Trinidad and Cape Town. She anchored in Sydney Harbour in mid-April to be stripped of all her luxurious fittings, and converted for use as a troop transport. At Sydney she was joined by the *Mauretania*, and other big liners gathered there to act as troop transports. On May 5th, 1940, the *Queen Mary* took on board the first 5,000 Australian and New Zealand troops and her vital role as a troopship had begun. Ten months later the *Queen Elizabeth* arrived in Sydney to be re-fitted and in April 1941 the two *Queens* had a Pacific reunion when they took to the sea together sailing for Suez in convoy. Throughout the summer of 1941 the two liners continued their trooping service without respite and by December they had carried 80,000 troops across the Pacific and Indian Oceans, reinforcing the British army in the Middle East Desert War.

With the Japanese attack on Pearl Harbour and America's entry into the war the role of the two *Queens* was seen in a different light, and as a result of the Anglo-American alliance and a meeting in Washington between Winston Churchill and President Roosevelt, the two sisters became G.I. ferries; it was left to Washington to decide how to use them. When fitted out as troop transports in Australia accommodation had been prepared for around 5,000 soldiers for each ship with wooden bunks in the state rooms and cabins, and hammocks in the public rooms. Once in American hands

The *Queen Mary* at war: the hospital had been the peacetime ballroom where 500 couples could dance. These sick and wounded men were going home to America.

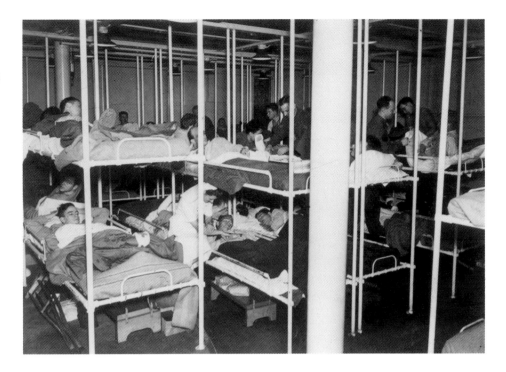

the sky was the limit and the two liners were re-fitted to take three times the number of troops previously carried. This was achieved by installing bunks in every available space, an American invention made of tubular metal uprights, with hinged tubular frames attached, over which strips of canvas were stretched with rope lacings. When not used the beds would be hinged upwards, and secured to the bulkhead or deckhead with a small chain and hook. Every available space was taken – the cocktail bars, cabins and even the drained swimming pools. Two shifts of G.I.s every twenty-four hours squeezed into the metal racks.

Transporting the equivalent of one army division per liner across the Atlantic under the hazard of enemy attack, time after time, in all weather conditions, was an appalling risk, but the Americans had confidence that the *Queens* would do the job and 'deliver the goods'. And so they did. From the time the Americans came in, the *Queen Mary* and *Queen Elizabeth* spent the remainder of the war trooping, mostly on the North Atlantic run with Gourock at the mouth of the Clyde the eastern terminus. On one westbound voyage the *Queen Elizabeth* transported 4,000 wounded soldiers accompanied by 400 doctors and nurses. On some America-bound crossings she was loaded with war prisoners. All told the *Elizabeth* made thirty-four round trips on the North Atlantic, mostly between New York and the River Clyde, and her sister, the *Mary* did twenty-eight.

On three occasions during the war the *Queen Mary* carried Prime Minister Winston Churchill from England to America with the Chiefs of Staff. On one trip, in May 1943, Churchill was accompanied by 5,000 German prisoners of war. The Prime Minister's quarters were, of course, *135*

The *Queen Mary* at war:
(*Left*) The tourist nursery
was the R.A.F. orderly room;
(*Left, below*) British and
U.S. gunners, who manned
the ship's armament, 'closing
up' at the double during an
exercise.

U.S. troops returning to New York on board H.M.S. *Queen Elizabeth*. R.A.F. planes flew past as the ship departed to New York from Southampton.

completely sealed off from the rest of the liner and had been restored to pre-war comfort with an added suite of offices and guard rooms which, for the duration of each voyage, became Britain's war headquarters. Chiefs of Staff, Cabinet Ministers, cipher clerks, detectives, bodyguards, Churchill's secretaries, including his daughter, Mary, all had their own offices and state rooms in the ship.

During the Yalta Conference held at the Crimean coastal town in February 1945 to make plans for the final defeat of Germany and attended by Churchill, Roosevelt and Stalin, Churchill lived aboard the *Franconia*. In the bathroom of *Franconia*'s Imperial Suite, Cunard carpenters had constructed a special wooden 'desk' that straddled the bath so that the Prime Minister could work at his papers as he bathed. He spent so much time at his work that he used to depress a call button with his toe to summon a steward to replenish the hot water when it became cold. Another special feature in Churchill's suite in *Franconia* was a plumber's candle that burned each night in a saucerful of water next to his bed. Its purpose? To light a nocturnal cigar.

In 1946, Churchill travelled again to the United States, this time in the *Queen Elizabeth* in the company of 12,000 triumphant G.I.s returning home. The G.I.s cheered him when he boarded the liner and they had further cause for cheers when, the day before they reached New York, he treated them to a typical Churchillian oration. This was what he said:

'My friends and shipmates in the *Queen Elizabeth*. For most of you it is homeward-bound. The seas are clear, the old flag flies and those who have done the work turn home again, their task accomplished, their duty done.

'What a strange, fearful yet glittering chapter this war has been!

'What changes it has wrought throughout the world, and in the fortunes of so many families! What an interruption in all the plans each of us had made! What a surrender of liberties we prized! What a casting away of comfort and safety! What a pride in peril! What a glory shines on the brave and the true!

'The good cause has not been overthrown. Tyrants have been hurled from their place of power, and those who sought to enslave the future of mankind have paid, or will pay, the final penalty . . .

'Yesterday I was on the bridge, watching the mountainous waves and this ship, which is no pup, cutting through them and mocking their anger. I asked myself, why is it that the ship beats the waves, when there are so many and the ship is one?

'The reason is that the ship has a purpose, and the waves have none. They just flop around, innumerable, tireless, but ineffective. The ship with the purpose takes us where we want to go. Let us therefore have purpose in our national and imperial policy, and in our private lives. Thus the future will be fruitful for each and for all, and the reward of the warriors will not be unworthy of the deeds they have done!'

PART THREE

1946-1987

Construction of the *Queen Elizabeth* (I).

(*Previous page*) The second *Caronia* – known as 'The Green Goddess' – was a great success as a cruise ship.

CHAPTER ELEVEN

Not the Only Way to Cross

After the end of the Second World War, the economic storm cones were hoisted on both sides of the Atlantic and the shipping world had much to do to repair the ravages of war. Once the war was over, Cunard had first to obtain the release of those of their ships that had survived from government control, and re-equip and re-employ them as revenue-earners in peacetime commercial service. This wasn't going to be easy, for the estimated charges for the re-conditioning of the *Queen Elizabeth*, *Queen Mary*, *Mauretania* and *Britannic* were £7,600,000, of which Cunard had to bear £2,250,000. In addition it was estimated that Cunard would have to fund £25 million of replacement costs for new ships to replace those lost during the war by Cunard and associated companies.

Sharply rising building costs did not help. A 10,500-ton cargo ship had cost Cunard £160,000 to build in 1925. To replace the ship in 1948 would cost £625,000. And a passenger liner like one of the *Queens*, which cost around £6 million each to build pre-war, would cost at least £15 million.

The company was also hit by the sudden death of the dynamic chairman, Sir Percy Bates, in 1946, just before the *Queen Elizabeth* sailed from Southampton on the maiden voyage she had to forgo in 1940. Sir Percy was the man who had made the *Queens* possible and on the maiden voyage of the *Elizabeth*, the captain, Sir James Bisset, held a memorial service for him marked by the liner's dance band playing his favourite hymn, 'Praise My Soul, the King of Heaven', and a short address by the captain:

'Shipmates and fellow voyagers, we are gathered to pay our respects to the memory of Sir Percy Bates, late chairman of the Cunard White Star Line, who died early in the morning of our departure from Southampton.

'Sir Percy Bates was mainly responsible for the building of these two great vessels, *Queen Mary* and *Queen Elizabeth*. He watched them grow, from masses of steel girders and plates, into the magnificent structures they are today. They were the children of his brain. He lived for them, he worked for them, he wore himself out with anxieties for them, and he has died for them.

'We who knew him, admired him, and loved him, have felt a shock of intense sorrow at his untimely passing – untimely, for he was to have been with us on this maiden voyage, and, like all of us in any way connected with this ship, he had looked forward with high hopes to its accomplishment. He loved the sea, he loved the ships, and he loved those who do business in the great waters.

'Here, in this ship, in mid-ocean, we remember him, with grief in our *141* hearts, and profound sympathy in our thoughts for Lady Bates and his sorrowing family and all the loved ones he had left behind.'

The financial situation in which Cunard White Star found itself soon after the Second World War was explained by Mr Frederick H. Bates, who had succeeded his brother, Sir Percy, as chairman. He told shareholders: 'When the cost of replacing an old ship has become three and four times the original something more than statutory allowance for depreciation before taxation is required. This can only come from profits the company may be able to make. These, after taxation at ten shillings in the pound, may be quite insufficient to replace the fleet, however much might be ploughed back into reserve.'

But around the table in the Cunard White Star boardroom there were some who considered that after six years of wartime travel restrictions there would be a new demand, not only for passengers across the Atlantic, but for tourist travel. And that those shipping companies able to get their act together and meet these demands could reap rich harvests. How was it to be done?

Members of the board were fairly confident that they could secure a reasonable amount of the immediate express traffic across the Atlantic with the two *Queens*, and some of the intermediate traffic with the *Mauretania* and *Britannic*. For a long-term policy, however, it was generally felt that shipbuilding plans involving changes of design for the New York and Canada trade would be necessary to satisfy passengers, the bulk of whom would be Americans. Further, new ships would be needed to meet an anticipated increase in the cruise business, and to retain Cunard's widespread cargo trade.

The *Queen Mary* was not 'demobbed' until September 1946, as she had been busy carrying tens of thousands of G.I.s back to America and had one more major task to perform – the transporting to America and Canada of some 25,000 European girl wives, mostly British, who had married American and Canadian servicemen, and 15,000 of their newborn babies. Between February and May 1946, the *Queen Mary* carried 12,886 G.I. brides and babies to New York while thousands of others were transported to Canada in the *Mauretania*, and on top of that were the royals, the dukes and duchesses, the millionaire tycoons and diplomats. Out came the 'standee' bunks from the *Queen Mary* and in went cots, nurseries and play rooms, and every time the liner docked in New York with her new Americans there were scenes in the harbour reminiscent of the famous maiden voyages with fire tenders spouting columns of water into the air, tug sirens blaring, planes flying overhead, and waiting G.I.s going nearly beserk on the dockside. The first reunions became more like scenes on the terraces of British football grounds in the 1980s as husbands broke down barriers and fought their way to get to their loved ones herded behind wire enclosures.

By 1947 the two *Queens*, overhauled and re-furnished, were ready to start Cunard's two-ship weekly shuttle service across the Atlantic for the first

G.I. brides with their babies on the way to their new homes in the *Queen Mary* after the war.

Before she was demobbed after the Second World War the *Queen Mary* carried thousands of American troops back to the United States.

time, and in July of that year the two great liners passed each other in their peacetime colours as they sailed round the Isle of Wight, the *Elizabeth* bound for New York, and the *Mary* coming into Southampton. From then on, for ten happy years, Cunard had passengers clamouring to sail in the *Queens*, each ship showing a gross profit of over £100,000 per round voyage. Some passengers were even happy to put down a deposit six months before a sailing date to secure the cabin of their choice. The optimists had been right, and there were much happier faces around the oak table on the fifth floor of the Cunard building at Liverpool's Pier Head

(*Right*) The *Queen Elizabeth* arriving at New York.

(*Above*) Her Majesty Queen Elizabeth with Sir Percy Bates inspecting the *Queen Elizabeth* on October 8th, 1946, shortly before the liner's maiden voyage.

at most board meetings.

Many famous people in the world travelled in the *Queens* during the post-war years. The Duke and Duchess of Windsor were frequent passengers between Cherbourg and New York. On one occasion seventy-five suitcases belonging to the couple were counted going into their luxurious suite aboard the *Queen Elizabeth* and a further seventy trunks put in the hold. On one of the last voyages of Sir James Bisset in the *Queen Elizabeth*, the Duke of Windsor asked him to his suite and surprised the Captain by telling him: 'I am sorry to hear that you will soon be retiring from the sea.' Sir James's impending retirement had been kept a close secret but somehow the Duke had found out and presented him with a pair of gold cuff-links as he wished him many happy years on the beach.

Post-war menus on the *Queens* became collectors' items and even the meals served near the end of the war on the *Queen Elizabeth*'s maiden voyage, whose passengers included Comrades Molotov and Vishinsky bound for the first session of the United Nations, caused eyebrows to be raised back in ration-book Britain. The dinner menu read: Grapefruit au Kirsch, Hors d'Oeuvres Variés. Soup – Consommé Royal, Cream of Mushroom. Fish – Red Mullet Meunière, Halibut Sauce Mousseline. Entrées – Croquette of Duckling, Tête de Veau Vinaigrette. Joint – Leg or Shoulder of Lamb with Mint Sauce. Vegetables – Green peas, Cauliflower. Potatoes – Boiled, Roast, Snow and Gaufrette. Relève – Roast Turkey, Chipolata Sauce, Salad – Salade Cressonière, Grill – Devilled Ham and 145

(*Left*) A young Queen Elizabeth with a young Prince Philip look down on an even younger film star, Roger Moore, passenger on the *Queen Mary*.

(*Above*) Life aboard the *Queen Elizabeth* before she was sold abroad and finally destroyed by fire in Hong Kong in 1972.

succotash. Sweets – Orange soufflé Pudding, Coupe Monte Carlo, Macedoine of Fruit Chantilly. Ices – Vanilla, Strawberry, Lemon, with Petit Fours. Fresh fruit and coffee.

Cunard forestalled adverse comment in British newspapers by explaining in a press release that all delicacies had been purchased in the United States and Canada, and Britain's contribution to the menus had just been potatoes and boiled fish.

But not all the rich and famous Cunard passengers wanted to feast on delicacies. Captain Robert 'Bob' Arnott, Chief Officer on *QE2* from her maiden voyage, who became captain in 1976, recalls that many preferred more simple and homely dishes to lobster from Maine, snails, caviar, grouse and Californian strawberries. The favourite shipboard banquet of Richard Burton and Elizabeth Taylor was English steak and kidney pie; Noel Coward often ordered bangers and mash (sausage and mashed potatoes); Kay Kendall, when travelling with her husband, Rex Harrison, preferred cottage pie; and the champion of gargantuan plain-eating at sea, Victor Mature, a frequent passenger on the *Queens*, would demolish a whole twelve-pound turkey at a sitting.

In one Cunard advertisement headed 'Will Your Requests Be As Outrageous as These?' a picture appeared showing a long queue of stewards carrying luggage aboard one of the *Queens* with the caption, ' "Take my bags," said the Duke of Windsor indicating 135 pieces of luggage'. A second picture, showing the contents of a dinner plate, carried the caption, 'A Texas millionaire ordered rattlesnake steaks for dinner. We did our best serving eels garnished with rattles.' 'Eccentric? Outrageous?' asked Cunard. 'You may think so but it's all in a day's work for the crew of a Cunard ship.' Reluctantly the advertisement added: 'Redecorating your room in your own colours (a duty we performed regularly for a certain duchess) is, sadly, a thing of the past. The whole oxen and herds of grilled antelope ordered by Commodore Sir James Charles (a former Captain of the *Carmania*, *Lusitania*, *Mauretania* and *Aquitania*, who became renowned for his lavish entertaining aboard) would also take a bit of rounding up today!'

In the 1940s and 50s the passenger lists of both *Queens* read like a Hollywood 'Who's Who' of the day – Rita Hayworth, Joan Crawford, David Niven, Humphrey Bogart, Burt Lancaster, Spencer Tracy, Alan Ladd, Bing Crosby, Laurel and Hardy, Lili Palmer. . .it went on and on. On top of that were the royals, the dukes and duchesses, and the millionaire tycoons and diplomats.

Going further back into the past, Noel Coward, Ginger Rogers, James Cagney and Pat O'Brien had often graced the luxury suites of the *Queens*. Douglas Fairbanks brought Mary Pickford on one voyage. Tom Mix brought his famous horse and had it fitted with a Cunard life belt around its neck specially for the photographers. Athlete Lord Burghley brought his running shoes, and Frances Day brought her Rolls Royce and her own hens so she could be sure of fresh eggs for breakfast. It was one of Cunard's boasts that they had carried everyone from Mark Twain to the Duke of Windsor, and a certain titled passenger once remarked to a duchess, 'Going Cunard is a state of grace!'

Lord Northcliffe, the newspaper proprietor and a frequent Cunard passenger, enthused that Cunard's food and wine was of a kind unobtainable anywhere but in a few top London West End restaurants.

And it wasn't all that long ago that Beatrice Lillie, who spent most of her life as a revue actress between New York and London, first gazed up at one of the *Queens* in Southampton Docks, and asked: 'When does this place get to New York?'.

*   *   *

147

It was not only the success of the *Queens* that helped Cunard over the post-war difficulties. The company was also helped by securing control of the whole of Cunard White Star and by December 1949 the merger between Cunard and White Star ceased to exist. Henceforth the conduct of business reverted back exclusively to The Cunard Steam-Ship Company Limited.

A long-term building programme was implemented and involved three new cargo liners, *Asia* (II), *Arabia* (III) and *Assyria*; two new intermediate-type liners with first-class only accommodation and hold space for 7,000 tons of cargo, *Media* and *Parthia*; and the re-building internally of *Ascania* (II). The *Media* and *Parthia* became Cunard's first post-war passenger ships.

Finally, *Caronia* (II) (some 34,000 tons gross) was built as a dual-purpose vessel with first and cabin classes only. Aimed at the North Atlantic service during the summer season, and dollar-earning world cruises at other times of the year, *Caronia* was described by Cunard as the first purpose-built cruise ship. Put into service in 1948 she became known as 'The Green Goddess' because her hull was painted four shades of green. She was also an overnight success. Built at John Brown's on the Clyde, she was launched on October 30th, 1947, by Princess Elizabeth, and a year later the Duke of Edinburgh sailed in her during coastal trials between the Clyde and Southampton. She had the tallest single mast and largest funnel afloat and needed a crew of 700 to look after 500 passengers.

Some people thought it was unfortunate that the *Caronia* had provision for only first and cabin class and no cargo capacity, but she became a most popular ship and cruised all over the world at a maximum speed of 22 knots, mostly out of New York, with occasional trans-Atlantic voyages to Southampton and Le Havre.

One of her captains, Captain Geoffrey Marr, said after leaving her: ' "The Green Goddess" was a beautiful ship, a symbol of luxury and leisure, and all her days were happy days; her ship's company were beyond reproach, and all were proud to sail in her as she followed the sun.' In the travel world it is often said that one can judge a good hotel by the length of time staff stayed, and if this could be said for ships, *Caronia* was a very good ship. Her crews stayed in her year after year because they liked the ship, the life and the type of passengers she carried. On board often six months at a time, they created a social life of their own and the *Caronia* Social and Athletic Club was one of the best supported in the shipping world. Sadly, *Caronia* only lasted twenty years.

The possibility that the aeroplane would one day compete with ships in the passenger and cargo-carrying business was first seen as a threat on Sunday, June 15th, 1919, when John Alcock and Arthur Whitten-Brown, both wartime aviators, became the first to fly non-stop across the Atlantic. Their converted Vimy bomber, built by Vickers at Brooklands, Weybridge, flew from a field at St John's, Newfoundland, to Ireland, in sixteen hours, twenty-eight minutes.

Before the First World War the chances of bridging the Atlantic by air had appeared as remote as flying to the moon. But during that war the aeroplane had developed so rapidly that by 1919 it was just a matter of who would be first to prepare a plane with the required range, and strike the right kind of weather. Alcock and Brown in their plane, which had really been built to bomb Berlin, changed for ever man's notion of time and distance and within a short time of their triumph the Vickers Vimy had been converted into a passenger-carrying plane. The Cunard board was aware of possible competition from air traffic from then on and, in 1934, under Sir Percy Bates's chairmanship, efforts were made to secure Cunard's interest in this new element, with the assumption that sea and air traffic across the Atlantic could one day prove complementary to each other. But Sir Percy could not arouse interest and his efforts proved abortive.

Development of the aeroplane leapt ahead during the Second World War, and with the coming of the jet age Cunard at last realized that if they were to survive, then their pre-war image would require drastic change. It was obvious that when a jet could take a passenger across the Atlantic almost before one of the *Queens* could undock and come up to speed out at sea, they would have to build ships in which to entertain people as well as transport them.

By 1957, with the number of people crossing the Atlantic by sea declining rapidly, the airlines began to outcarry the ships, and the introduction of jets brought the journey down to seven hours. The jets had a further advantage – they could fly above the bad weather. In the mid-'fifties the passenger side of Cunard had been earning £32 million a year. Yet, within a decade, as the number of people crossing the Atlantic by air reached 8 million a year, Cunard passenger ships were showing a serious financial loss. Ships could no longer compete with aircraft either in speed or price. Something had to be done if Cunard were to survive the threat from the air, and, in the end, plucking at straws, the company fell back on the old maxim, 'If you can't beat 'em, join 'em,' and moved into the growth industry of trans-Atlantic air travel.

Firstly, in 1959, they acquired the independent airline, Eagle Airways Ltd, together with associated companies, and set up a subsidiary company, Cunard Eagle. Eagle Airways had developed an extensive network of scheduled services in Europe and were also operating a wide network of services in the western hemisphere and had government approval to operate on the route from London to Nassau in the Bahamas. Next they attempted to get authority to fly the Atlantic independently from London to New York and bought two Boeing aircraft. They managed to obtain a licence but in 1961 this was revoked by the Minister of Aviation and alternative employment had to be found for the two Boeings.

Currently with the acquisition of British Eagle, Cunard had entered into discussions with B.O.A.C. (British Overseas Airways Corporation) with the idea of doing a deal so that passengers could travel one way by sea *149* and one way by air and qualify for the return ticket discount. In June 1962 an agreement was reached in which Cunard invested £8½ million to take up a 30 per cent interest in B.O.A.C. and form B.O.A.C. – Cunard Ltd.

After initial losses, the air venture started to yield profits, building up through 1964 and 1965, but the National Union of Seamen's strike of 1966, which disrupted the whole shipping industry, cost Cunard £4 million, and once again the company was looking for assets to sell to make good the cash loss. Cunard–Eagle Airways was sold back to the original owner. But this was not enough. Left with inescapable capital commitments, including having to pay their share to invest in necessary new long-haul jets at £8 million each, the Cunard board had no alternative but also to realize their investment in B.O.A.C.–Cunard Ltd. Negotiations took place in August and September 1966 and resulted in the sale of Cunard's interest in B.O.A.C. for £11½ million in cash, giving them a profit on the original deal of £3 million.

Cunard's attempt to achieve and maintain an interest in air travel was back to square one.

Working quietly behind the scenes to find a future for Cunard on the sea against the growing supremacy of air traffic was the last of the three Bates brothers to become head of the company, Colonel Denis Haughton Bates, M.C. Col. Bates, very much a backroom boy who never sought the limelight of publicity and who used to drive himself to work in a Morris Minor, had taken over as chairman from his brother Frederick in 1953, and had been on the board since 1941. In addition to being chairman of the Cunard Steam-Ship Company he was also chairman of Brocklebanks, and on the board of Port Line. Col. Bates was committed to the belief that a new *Queen* was the answer to Cunard's troubles.

During the late 1950s rapid advances had been made in shipbuilding technology, and when ideas began to be formulated for the eventual replacement of the *Queen Mary* and *Queen Elizabeth*, technological progress enabled designers greatly to exceed what had previously been achieved. But before even a start could be made on a new design for a *Queen*, government financial help would again be needed – a plan which aroused hostility from other big ship-owners.

Nevertheless, Col. Bates went ahead with his negotiations with the government. At the turn of the century, Cunard had received a government loan of £2,600,000 towards the building of the *Lusitania* and *Mauretania*. For the *Queen Mary* they had borrowed £3 million, and for the *Queen Elizabeth*, £5,000,000. All this money had been repaid on time. So once again Cunard asked the government for a loan and not a subsidy, and on behalf of his company Col. Bates pleaded for help on the grounds of prestige, stressing that it was important for Britain that big ships should maintain the Atlantic express service if the company was to survive. He also maintained that the company had paid so much in taxation over the years that it deserved a loan.

150   Some newspapers did not appear to be on Cunard's side, however, and

the *Observer* came out with an article headed 'WHO IS CUNARD KIDDING?' commenting: 'If courage alone produced profits Cunard would have little to worry about. In five short years Cunard's passenger liners have lost £14.1 million in the troubled waters of the Atlantic. Yet, Cunard believes there is profit in passengers and sailors on.'

In September 1959, 48 hours after the government had announced it would set up an independent committee to advise on the replacement of the *Queen Mary* and the *Queen Elizabeth*, Col. Bates, aged 73, suffered a heart attack and died at his home at Chorlton Hall, in Cheshire. The night before he died he had invited his son, Philip, also a Cunard director, to dinner and had been in great form talking about a fine successor planned for the *Queens*.

Under the heading 'THE ENIGMA OF CUNARD DIES', the *Daily Mail* came out the day after the death of Colonel Bates with the following:

Three quirks of his nature made him a puzzle.

He gave gracious living to millions aboard his ships, yet he lived a spartan, almost a recluse's life.

He persuaded the same millions that cruises and business trips by sea were just the thing. Yet he went to sea only twice during his six years as chairman.

He had to see that his company was in the forefront. Yet his aversion to self-advertisement was so strong that he refused to have his name in 'Who's Who' – 'Tell them to mind their own business,' he said.

Bates, the spartan, was horrified at the thought of a chauffeur and an imposing Rolls, so he drove himself in a Morris Minor from his home, Chorlton Hall, near Malpas, Cheshire, 34 miles to his Liverpool office every morning.

Each evening he drove home to more work. He and his wife had no servants, took no part in the town's life, entertained only relatives and close friends.

But when the Bellringers of Malpas heard about his death they suggested a muffled peal before morning service. The Rector, the Rev. Thomas Rylands, vetoed it – 'Because he hated special attention.'

Sir John Brocklebank, Bt, of the Brocklebank shipping family, reluctantly succeeded Col. Bates as Cunard chairman; shortly a new *Queen* went on the drawing board called the Q4 (an earlier Q3 had been abandoned) and in 1963 Sir John announced that an agreement with the government had been signed under which a maximum of £17,600,000 would be made available at $4\frac{1}{2}$ per cent.

The Q4 was then designed as a ship capable of following the sun, and included in her anticipated itineraries were many ports that her deep-draughted predecessors had been incapable of entering. Her size of 65,000 tons gross would still make her one of the world's largest passenger liners but her draught and dimensions would give her access to more ports with a 151 marketing appeal. So the *QE 2* was conceived – the first large British liner planned as a 'resort hotel' to capture the cream of the North Atlantic trade in the season, and the cream of the sun-seeking leisure class in the winter. It was a step in the dark and once again Cunard were going into unknown regions.

Cunard had estimated that it would cost £22 million to build the *QE 2* but when the contract was signed with John Brown of Clydebank the cost had gone up to £25,427,000. To raise the extra cash and to provide immediate funds, Cunard were forced to mortgage five of their passenger liners and six cargo ships – the government loan was not to be provided until the ship had actually been delivered. Cunard also borrowed from a consortium of British bankers up to £17,600,000 at a rate of a ½ per cent over the bank rate, with a minimum of 5 per cent per year.

When the contract was finally signed, *The Times* commented: 'What Cunard has embarked on is a unique compromise between express liner and cruise ship. No one has attempted it before. It remains to be seen whether the two are commercially reconcilable. This ship is genuinely an act of faith and courage. The country will applaud both owners and builders and wish them well.'

In 1964 Cunard announced that Sir Basil Smallpeice, K.C.V.O., had joined the Cunard board from B.O.A.C. Sir Basil had resigned from B.O.A.C. after thirteen years and it was ironic that he should be called in by Sir John Brocklebank to help save the passenger shipping business which he had done much as an airline chief to undermine. Shortly afterwards Sir John Brocklebank stood down as Cunard chairman due to ill health, and was succeeded as Chairman by Sir Basil; he was soon sweeping through the company like a new broom and attempting a full-scale rescue operation. One of his first positive steps was to call in a leading firm of management consultants to improve the organization with a widespread brief. Then the Economist Intelligence Unit (E.I.U.) was asked to conduct a thorough study of the travel and cruise markets of passenger ships.

In 1965 the reports on Cunard's affairs from the management consultants, Urwick, Orr and Partners, the E.I.U. and from Professor A.R. Ilersic of London University were sent to the company. These recommended, as top priority, that Cunard should get its passenger fleet back on a paying, or at least a break-even basis, in which cruising should play an important part. The reports also suggested that the company should rationalize the cargo operations of the group to greater advantage, and seek out other profitable fields of enterprise in which to expand or diversify activities and resources.

The E.I.U. report also contained an uncompromising warning that without drastic re-development the company was on the verge of an exceptionally serious financial crisis. The management consultants emphasized that any decision to remain in the passenger business must be coupled with a decision to embark on a major re-organization which would require firm direction and sustained determination at all levels.

The main recommendations were acted upon immediately and included a drastic rationalization of the Cunard fleet including the sale of the *Mauretania*, *Queen Mary* and *Queen Elizabeth*; the moving of the management of the passenger ships of the future from Liverpool to Southampton; and the re-organization of the company into five main divisions, with Mr Philip Bates, the 40-year-old son of the late Col. Denis Bates, as managing director. The five divisions were: commercial, hotel, technical, personnel and accounting.

The new chairman explained:

'It is only when we fully grasp the significance of the altered role of passenger shipping in an air-dominated world that we see the dawn of hope for the future.

'For then, the new ship (the *QE2*) will no longer be thought of as the last of the great line of large passenger transport vehicles, but as the first of a great line of great ships in the floating hotel or resort business. Once it is realised that this is our role in the future, we are faced no longer with eking out a bare existence in the last decade or two of passenger sea transport, but with the prospect of developing and expanding the vacation industry at sea.'

By 1966 a complete new policy had been evolved for the passenger ship side of the company to overcome the adverse financial and trading conditions – not a new situation in the long history of Cunard. Sir Basil Smallpeice explained that the keynote of this new policy would be that in terms of marketing concepts a passenger ship should no longer be regarded as a means of transport, 'but even more as a floating resort in which people take a holiday and enjoy themselves'. By so altering the function of the passenger ship the company would then no longer be in a contracting market but in a growth industry – leisure.

'This is an industry which is undergoing great expansion in which our share will be limited only by the economics of ships and the prices we have to charge to make them profitable,' said Sir Basil.

But before the function of Cunard passenger ships could be changed to 'floating resorts' the old had to go to help pay for the new. In 1967, the *Queen Mary* was sold to the highest bidder, which turned out to be the City of Long Beach, California, who paid £1,240,000 for her to be used as a maritime museum. She arrived at Southampton from New York on September 27th, 1967, completing her 1,000th voyage, and on October 31st sailed to America's west coast where today she lies at Long Beach serving as a conference and tourist centre.

Her last voyage to Long Beach was a remarkable one in so far as she became the first of the *Queens* to round Cape Horn and become a 'Cape Horner'. The voyage, with 1,300 American passengers flown to England to start the journey of 15,000 miles, lasted 39 days. In command was Captain John Treasure Jones, one of the great characters Cunard had the happy knack of choosing as captains. Accompanying him was his wife, Belle, one of the first Cunard wives ever allowed to sail with her husband whilst in command.

Captain Treasure Jones who took the *Queen Mary* on her last voyage around Cape Horn.

This too was to be a last major voyage for Captain Jones (Treasure was a family name and nothing to do with an explanation often given by the captain to enquirers that on his birth his mother looked on him and said, 'What a little Treasure!'). After $31\frac{1}{2}$ years with Cunard, Captain Jones was to retire the following year.

When eighteen years later he talked of the *Mary*'s last trip around the Cabo de Hornos, still feared by sailors and the graveyard of many a fine ship, he was a fit and lively 81 years of age and still playing eighteen holes of golf.

'I thoroughly enjoyed every moment of the trip,' he said. 'Cape Horn produced no real problem. It was a lovely day and we had a moderate north easterly blowing us round. I passed within one and a half miles. It was the closest I could get as there were quite a few rocks around me. I took some good pictures of the Horn with a blanket of cloud over her top.

'When I got back home, Sir Alex Rose who had just sailed round the world on his own, was the principal speaker at a 'Cape Horners' Dinner' at which I too was a guest and he asked me how far off Cape Horn I had passed in the *Queen Mary*. When I said "Within a mile and a half," he was astonished and answered, "I passed at least twenty miles off. I didn't want to see it, just get round it!".'

Captain Jones chose to go round Cape Horn because the *Queen Mary* was too large to pass through the Panama Canal; the route was Southampton, Las Palmas, Rio de Janeiro, Cape Horn, Valparaiso, Callao

(Peru), Balboa, Acapulco, Long Beach.

The route caused problems with supplies of both fresh water and fuel. The *Queen Mary* was built to carry a supply of up to 7 days' worth of fresh water for the five-day Atlantic crossing plus a further 200 tons a day for the 24 boilers. She also burned 1,100 tons of oil a day.

'The trouble was that the only ports the *Queen Mary* could get alongside for water and fuel on our route to Long Beach were at Las Palmas and Balboa at the western end of the Panama Canal,' explained Captain Jones.

'We got round conserving fresh water by running just the first class dining room for the passengers with two sittings instead of the usual two dining rooms, and the cabin class dining room was used for all the crew instead of crew messes all around the ship. And the way we overcame the fuel problem was to go at reduced speed on two engines and only half the boilers. This cut down fuel consumption by half.'

At each of the major ports of call local officials were taken on board as guests for the next leg and on the last part of the journey from Valparaiso, the Mayor of Long Beach, whose city was footing the bill for the voyage and actually made a profit on it, was the principal guest.

Captain Jones added: 'Soon after the Mayor of Long Beach came on board he said to me, "Captain, I want as little as possible left in the ship when we get to Long Beach. As we are not allowed to land food in America or Havana cigars, and we don't want a lot of liquor left over, it is up to you to see that the passengers enjoy it all!" So, from Valparaiso on we were throwing cocktail parties every day and trying to drink up all the booze – champagne galore, as much as one could drink; all the caviare one could eat; and handfuls of the finest cigars to smoke before we reached Long Beach. There will never be a cruise like that again. I enjoyed it all the way.

'At Long Beach there was a reception waiting for us of about eight to ten thousand boats. The mayor had told us that all California would be out to see their *Queen Mary*. And it looked as if he was right. The mayor, wearing a Cunard sailor's hat on his head, came down the gangway with me.

'But when it came to handing over the ship and I had to sign the *Queen Mary* over to the City of Long Beach, and down came our flag, and up went the U.S. flag, and the Long Beach Flag went up in place of the Cunard House Flag – then, I really felt nostalgic and I shed a couple of tears. It was the end of the *Queen Mary*, and it was nearing the end of my seafaring career.'

The *Queen Elizabeth* was sold to a consortium of Philadelphia business-men who wanted to use her in Port Everglades, Florida, as a tourist attraction; when she finally left Southampton on November 29th, 1968, she had made 907 Atlantic crossings, steamed for 3,470,000 miles, and carried over 2.3 million people during her 28-year career. Before her last sailing, Her Majesty Queen Elizabeth, the Queen Mother, made a special journey from London to say a royal farewell to the ship she had launched over thirty years before, and to lunch with the Cunard board in the famed verandah grill.

The Florida venture failed and the liner was put up for auction when

(*Above*) The middle building is the Cunard building in Liverpool.

(*Left*) Ceiling in the lobby of 25 Broadway.

The *Queen Elizabeth* (I) on fire in Hong Kong.

C.Y. Tung, of Orient Overseas Line, paid £1,333,000 for her. The *Queen Elizabeth* was then renamed *Seawise University* and sailed to Hong Kong for conversion to a floating university. In January 1972, when work on her conversion was almost complete, fire broke out aboard. For three days the fire raged and when at last it was over, the grand old lady was completely gutted, and had to be totally written off.

In 1968 *Carinthia* (III) and *Sylvania* (II) were sold for a total of £2,450,000; *Caronia* was taken out of service because it would cost too much to convert her to modern cruising and was sold to the Star Shipping Company, Panama. In 1974, whilst being towed to the breakers in Taiwan, the 'Green Goddess' decided to bow out in her own way, broke adrift from her tow in heavy weather, and ran aground on the island of Guam in the Pacific, splitting into three pieces.

Other economies followed and Cunard offices were closed in Paris, Le Havre and Dublin. There were reductions in staff in London and Southampton, and the Cunard building in Liverpool, and the Port Line Building in Sydney, were sold for a total of £3.6 million. Perhaps the most famous building to be sold was No. 25 Broadway, New York; Leadenhall Street, London, was also sold.

One of the famous captains of both the *Queen Mary* and *Queen Elizabeth*, Commodore Geoffrey Marr, D.S.C., took the sale of the great Cunard liners and the subsequent reductions in personnel very much to heart. In his autobiography, *The Queens And I,* he told of the day in November 1967 when he had to assemble the ship's company of the *Queen Elizabeth*, and read to them the chairman's message telling them that, in addition to the two *Queens*, the *Caronia, Sylvania* and *Carinthia* were all to be withdrawn from service and put up for sale:

> In effect, Cunard was for sale. Thus 1957's greatest passenger fleet of the North Atlantic was within ten short years to be reduced to three ships. But it was what this meant in terms of human lives that was important, because within the space of a couple of months 2,700 men and women, many of them with a lifetime of service, were to lose their means of livelihood. It was certainly a grim time and, as the ships came into their home port, those on whom the axe was to fall were called in and told that it was a case of being given redundancy pay or taking early retirement.
>
> However one looks at it, the choice was bitter, and it seemed a poor reward to those who had in many cases devoted the whole of their working lives to the service of the once great Cunard line. It is a sad tale, but one that is too often retold in the business climate of today.

CHAPTER TWELVE

The Fun Way to the Sun

The idea of Cunard going into the business of liners to the sun was really nothing new; their ships had been taking people on cruising holidays since before the turn of the twentieth century. A Scotsman, Arthur Anderson, the founder of the *Shetland Journal*, is credited with having invented the idea of cruising in 1835 when he carried an advertisement in his newspaper headed 'To Tourists' which proposed a cruise around Iceland and the Faroe Islands. He didn't get many takers with such a forbidding itinerary, particularly as the date of the proposed sailing was mid-winter. But the idea was there.

Later in the century the Victorians discovered you could go on a ship, not just to reach a destination, but for the pure excitement and entertainment of a voyage, and cruising began to catch on. Today more than two million people take cruise holidays annually, with Americans topping the list followed by the British, Germans, rest of Europe, Australia, Canada and the Far East. More than 300 ports are visited each year by ships of the world's cruise lines with the Caribbean the most popular venue for warm-weather sailing and the Aegean and the Mediterranean not far behind.

Back at the start of it all, the Orient Line ran pleasure cruises in 1889 to the Mediterranean, the Norwegian Fjords and the West Indies, and the first official world cruise was offered by Cunard in 1922 on the *Laconia*. The *Laconia* (18,099 tons) could carry 2,200 passengers – more than most other liners of the day – and was a three-class ship which catered mainly for American sun-seekers and sailed from New York. The Americans found other uses for cruise ships during Prohibition days as only a few miles out at sea real liquor could be served in unlimited quantities, and many ships became known for their 'Booze Cruises'. Some say they haven't changed all that much.

From 1923 several cruise vessels owned by United States lines made east–west world cruises carrying up to 166 passengers encompassing both the Suez and Panama canals, the blue Pacific, Asia and Europe, on a 105-day voyage. Today, Cunard's *Queen Elizabeth 2*, the world's fastest passenger liner, accomplishes the same voyage in 89 days, at the same time allowing for the maximum amount of time in each port. By the 1930s, as more and more liners became floating hotels seeking out the more exotic places in the world for the millionaires to spend their money, cruising began to attract other kinds of people, rather than just the wealthy who often arrived aboard accompanied by their personal servants.

ROUND THE WORLD CRUISE, 1939

IN THE

PALATIAL WORLD - CRUISING LINER

" FRANCONIA " (20,000 TONS)

ITINERARY

Port	Miles	Arrive			Sail		
SOUTHAMPTON	—	—	—	—	Sat., Dec. 24	—
NEW YORK	3,000	Mon., Jan.	2,	—	Thur., Jan.	5,	00.05 am
PORT OF SPAIN	1,932	Tues., ,,	10,	6.00 am	Tues., ,,	10,	2.00 pm
RIO DE JANEIRO	3,136	Thur., ,,	19,	7.00 am	Fri., ,,	20,	Midnight
BUENOS AIRES	1,142	Tues., ,,	24,	6.00 am	Wed., ,,	25,	6.00 pm
MONTEVIDEO	125	Thur., ,,	26,	7.00 am	Thur., ,,	26,	Noon
CAPETOWN	3,649	Sun., Feb.	5,	Noon	Thur., Feb.	9,	5.00 pm
PORT ELIZABETH	422	Sat., ,,	11,	6.00 am	Sat., ,,	11,	5.00 pm
DURBAN	396	Mon., ,,	13,	6.00 am	Thur., ,,	16,	5.00 pm
ZANZIBAR	1,607	Tues., ,,	21,	6.00 am	Tues., ,,	21,	6.00 pm
MOMBASA	132	Wed., ,,	22,	6.00 am	Wed., ,,	22,	5.00 pm
PORT VICTORIA	969	Sat., ,,	25,	8.30 am	Sat., ,,	25,	1.30 pm
BOMBAY	1,752	Thur., Mar.	2,	8.30 am	Thur., Mar.	9,	6.00 pm
COLOMBO	889	Sun., ,,	12,	6.00 am	Tues., ,,	14,	6.00 pm
BELAWAN DELI	1,240	Sat., ,,	18,	6.00 am	Sat., ,,	18,	6.00 pm
PENANG	145	Sun., ,,	19,	8.00 am	Mon., ,,	20,	5.00 am
SINGAPORE	393	Tues., ,,	21,	8.00 am	Tues., ,,	21,	6.00 pm
PAKNAM	811	Fri., ,,	24,	2.00 am	Fri., ,,	24,	9.00 pm
TOURANE	1,134	Tues., ,,	28,	5.00 am	Tues., ,,	28,	7.00 pm
HONG KONG	519	Thur., ,,	30,	7.00 am	Fri., ,,	31,	5.00 pm
MANILA	630	Sun., April	2,	11.00 am	Mon., April	3,	2.00 am
BATAVIA	1,562	Fri., ,,	7,	8.00 am	Sat., ,,	8,	2.30 pm
SEMARANG	236	Sun., ,,	9,	2.00 pm	Sun., ,,	9,	2.00 pm
PADANG BAY (Bali)	423	Tues., ,,	11,	6.00 am	Wed., ,,	12,	5.00 pm
KUPANG (Timor)	503	Fri., ,,	14,	6.00 am	Fri., ,,	14,	5.00 pm
PORT DARWIN	475	Sun., ,,	16,	6.00 am	Sun., ,,	16,	4.00 pm
PORT MORESBY (Papua)	1,081	Thur., ,,	20,	1.00 am	Thur., ,,	20,	9.00 pm
FILA (New Hebrides)	1,340	Mon., ,,	24,	1.00 pm	Mon., ,,	24,	6.00 pm
NOUMEA (New Caledonia)	328	Wed., ,,	26,	6.00 am	Wed., ,,	26,	Noon
SUVA (Fiji)	730	Fri., ,,	28,	2.00 pm	Sat., ,,	29,	3.00 am
NUKUALOFA (Friendly Is.)	436	Sun., ,,	30,	10.00 am	Sun., ,,	30,	5.00 pm
PAGO PAGO (E. Samoa)	490	Mon., May	1,	6.00 am	Mon., May	1,	5.00 pm
APIA (W. Samoa)	88	Tues., ,,	2,	5.00 am	Tues., ,,	2,	1.00 pm
HONOLULU	2,262	Mon., ,,	8,	4.00 pm	Tues., ,,	9,	2.00 pm
SAN FRANCISCO	2,091	Mon., ,,	15,	10.00 am	Tues., ,,	16,	10.00 am
BALBOA	3,246	Thur., ,,	25,	6.00 am	Thur., ,,	25,	Noon
CRISTOBAL	44	Thur., ,,	25,	8.00 pm	No stop		
NEW YORK	1,972	Wed., ,,	31,	8.00 am	Fri., June	2,	—
LIVERPOOL	3,000	Mon., ,,	12,	—	—	—	—
	44,330						

Subject to Alteration

RATES FROM 410 GNS.

(Including Standard Shore Excursions).

(*Left*) Table of cruise prices, 1939.

(*Right, above*) H.M.S. *Queen Mary* painted in battleship grey from the *Queen Elizabeth* in the Indian Ocean in 1941; artist Frank Norton.

(*Right, below*) Painted battleship grey, the *Aquitania* at sea in the Indian Ocean during her years at a troop transport; artist Frank Norton.

In Britain, cotton workers from the Lancashire mills discovered they could cruise to the Mediterranean from Liverpool with Cunard for just 17 guineas (£17 17s) for thirteen days. Cunard White Star were advertising at the same time a 22-day cruise in the *Lancastria* to Gibraltar, Tangier, Villefranche and Lisbon for 22 guineas; and at the start of 1939 one could take a 52-day cruise in the *Laconia* calling at Santa Cruz, Dakar, Rio de Janeiro, Bahia, Port of Spain, Curacao, Cristobal, Kingston, Nassau, Miami, Madeira, from 100 guineas.

Cunard White Star's 'Round the World' cruise in 1939 in the 'palatial

(*Previous page*) Cutaway and exterior shots of the *QE2*.

(*Left*) Crew and staff of the liner *QE2* assemble on the main deck for an historic picture, taken in New York before her last voyage under steam: 1,100 people, and not the entire crew (80 were keeping the ship 'ticking' below).

(*Right*) Quoits on the deck of the *Franconia*.

world-cruising liner', *Franconia*, starting at Southampton in January and finishing at Liverpool in the following June, would only set one back 410 guineas, including shore excursions: it would take you to Rio, Capetown, Zanzibar, Bombay, Penang, Singapore, Hong Kong, Manila, Bali, Papua, Fiji, the Friendly Islands, Honolulu, San Francisco and New York.

But with these amazingly economical fares one had to pay for rugs and cushions for your deck chairs on the sun deck. A notice in the *Lancastria* told passengers:

> Deck chairs are supplied free of charge. Rugs and cushions can be hired at a charge of two shillings and sixpence each on application to the deck steward. The hire of rugs and/or cushions will entitle passengers to retain the exclusive use of the chairs on which the rug and/or cushions are placed. Each rug is contained in a sealed cardboard box, and bears a serial number worked into the material so that passengers will have no difficulty in identifying their rugs. At the end of each voyage, the rugs which have been in use are sent to the store and thoroughly cleaned before being re-issued.

This must have made the passengers from the Lancashire cotton mills feel really at home – just like Blackpool during Wakes Week.

The assistant cruise director with Cunard White Star in the mid-'thirties was Old Etonian Sir Charles Baring, who sailed on a number of cruises in the *Lancastria*. At the age of 87 Sir Charles recalled how cruising suddenly   *165*

(*Left, above*) The garden lounge of the *Franconia*. A round-the-world cruise in *Franconia* could cost as little as 410 guineas.

(*Left, below*) the gymnasium of the *Franconia*.

Captain Robert Harry Arnott, an early master of the *QE2*, well remembers his cruising days.

became very popular in those days.

'It wasn't surprising,' he said. 'The public began to realize that you could cruise in a Cunard ship to the West Indies with excellent first-class accommodation for £120 and the rush started.

'The *Lancastria* was essentially a north country ship and sailed out of Liverpool and many of the first passengers I had to look after were on holiday from the cotton mills and used to arrive on deck in their clogs.

'Cruising saved the day for shipping in the mid-'thirties although a number of senior officers, both sea-going and ashore, thought it was beneath them and did their best to deride it. There were captains too who didn't like the idea.'

Sir Charles was high in his praise for Cunard crews.

'The crews were generally hand-picked and the discipline in Cunard ships was much tighter than in any other line. Any drunkenness or incivility to passengers and you would be put ashore and paid off. Some thought the discipline was too strict but they stayed with the company because the pay was good.

'On the cruise ships I sailed on, the B.R.s (bedroom stewards) were some of the best paid. They were generally older men who had a wonderful way with passengers. Many people who first came aboard were afraid of the sea and were determined they were going to be ill. It was down to the B.R.s to get them out of their bunks and on deck and they really did a good job and earned their money.'

Sir Charles became Cruise Director on the White Star liner, *Doric*, in 1935, which had been taken over by Cunard in the merger with White Star.

'I can never understand why Cunard bothered to take her over,' said Sir Charles. 'She was one of the last coal-burning ships, very unpopular, and far below the standard set by Cunard.'

The *Doric* wasn't to last long under Cunard. One night in September 1935 off Finisterre, Sir Charles had retired to his cabin about 23.00, and looking out of his porthole he saw a large French ship without lights about to cross the *Doric*'s bows.

'I had a first-class view of what happened next,' he said. 'She hit us on the starboard side almost mid-ships and her bows tore into the cabin accommodation of two of our young lady passengers who, as usual in cruising those days, were in other people's cabins and escaped! But I saw all the clothes belonging to the young ladies fall out of their wrecked cabin into the sea and go floating away.

'The *Doric* took on a list to starboard and I went to the bridge where the captain told me to get all the passengers lined up on deck as he was going to abandon ship.

'It was a nightmare rounding up the passengers, mostly all north country people, but luckily the P. and O. ship *Viceroy* arrived on the scene, came alongside, and we transferred all 400 passengers.'

Captain 'Bob' Arnott of *QE 2*, who described himself a 'shipboard adviser to many of the Hollywood greats, to the world's political-chiefs, and   *167* father confessor to tens of thousands of ordinary folk who have travelled on my ships', well remembers cruising to the Caribbean in the *Mauretania* as senior second officer.

The *Mauretania* and the *Caronia* were the first world-cruise ships to be fully air conditioned and every cabin in the *Caronia* boasted a private adjoining bathroom.

'The mid-'fifties saw the real start of the cruising scene as we know it today,' Captain Arnott recalled. 'The huge jets of B.O.A.C., Pan Am and half a dozen European airlines were already lifting passengers by the thousands away from the cabins of trans-Atlantic liners, and Cunard saw clearly that future prosperity – and perhaps even sheer survival – would depend on a successful switch to cruising.

'The custom-built *Caronia* was already shipping travellers around the world's tourist resorts, and even before the war the *Franconia* had pioneered world cruises. Ships of the Holland–American Line were also getting into the cruising game. Their liner *Nieuw Amsterdam* was almost a double of *Mauretania*, and she often followed our creamy wake through the blue Caribbean in whistle-stop tours of the islands. For passengers, cruising in the sun was a luxury pleasure, but for Cunard's ocean giants the sombre choice was between cruising and the breaker's yard.'

In New York, where the *Mauretania* started her sun cruises in the 'fifties, four of her lifeboats were taken away to make room for special cruise launches needed for landing passengers at ports in the Caribbean too small to take *Mauretania* to the quayside. Then she set off for the islands of Aruba, Curacao and St Martin, and on to the breathtaking vista of Puerto Rico's San Juan Bay.

On one occasion the American Liquor Dealers took over the *Mauretania* for a sales incentive cruise and the booze barons brought their own stocks aboard in bottles, barrels and tanks.

'I don't think I have ever seen so much liquor sloshing around one ship,' recollected Captain Arnott, who first went to sea at the age of seventeen. 'So many parties were going on during the cruise that no one, it seemed, ever finished a drink. So much wasted liquor was poured down the ship's drains by stewards that one of them swore to me that he had heard a following school of dolphins hiccuping all over the Caribbean!'

Derek Garner, a former wine steward and barman on Cunard cruise ships, was in at the start of the 'Cruise Now, Pay Later' era which began in America in the 1950s, became popular with credit-encouraged citizens of the United States, and was taken up by Cunard with voyages starting from New York. Mr Garner, now a successful international business executive, spends a great deal of his time today flying around the world, but he will never forget the start of his life as a young man at sea serving drinks to Cunard cruise passengers, mostly Americans.

'The Americans were wonderful customers, mainly because of their pride in the Cunard line which they genuinely considered was part of the heritage of the United States,' said Derek Garner. 'They were also most appreciative of Cunard service. They were great supporters of the Cunard line and still are to this day. They loved the grandeur and magnificence of the big ships and marvelled at the extravagant brilliance of the interior decor.

'The ships' officers played a great part in shipboard life and when not on sea duty they were encouraged to mix freely with the passengers. They were great ambassadors both for Cunard and their country.'

Born in Liverpool, Derek Garner served aboard three of Cunard's cruise ships working out of New York – the ex-White Star motorship *Britannic*, launched in 1929; *Parthia* (13,362 tons) launched in 1948 and accommodating 251 first class passengers; and the *Saxonia* (II) (21,637 tons), launched in 1954 by Lady Churchill, wife of the then Prime Minister, and re-named *Carmania* in 1963 when she was re-fitted for two-weekly cruises to the Caribbean from New York, and from Port Everglades in the winter. Sadly, in 1971, the *Saxonia/Carmania* was taken out of service after it was found she was costing too much in fuel and manning costs. To save money an attempt was made to introduce a foreign catering crew. This was strongly opposed by the unions and as a result the ship was sold to the Russian State Lines and became the *Leonid Sobinov*. At the same time, the *Franconia* was sold to the Russians as a cruise ship for £1 million and renamed *Fedor Shalyapin*.

By 1962 the golden years of the 'fifties had disappeared as far as cruising was concerned. Only the 'Green Goddess' (the *Caronia*) just about managed to continue paying her way. In Cunard's head office there were graphs at the time showing each ship's profits or losses. On the one for the *Caronia* the line plunged heavily into the red after the bill for an annual overhaul had been paid, then during a world cruise climbed slowly back, levelled off during a spring cruise, climbed again during a North Cape cruise, only to sink back towards the red during both the following summer and autumn cruises.

'But the overall picture of *Caronia*, the first Cunard ship designed purely for cruising, showed her to have been one of the most popular ships Cunard had ever built,' explained Philip Bates, whose great grandfather, Sir Edward Bates, a former Member of Parliament for Plymouth, Devon, formed the Bates Shipping Company in 1840 to run a tramp shipping service between Liverpool and India. Philip Bates, a Second World War captain in the Royal Marines serving in the 3rd Commando Brigade, started as an office boy in the Cunard Liverpool offices, married a lady assistant purser employed in the liner *Mauretania*, and went on to become deputy-chairman of the Cunard Steam-Ship Company.

'She had capacity for four hundred and fifty passengers, a crew requirement of between six hundred and seven hundred, and she was really known as the "Green Goddess" because she was the same colour as the Liverpool trams which were known as "Green Goddesses"!

'Eventually, *Caronia* earned the name "God's Waiting Room", because she attracted a lot of the old, the bold, and the wealthy. And when the Stock Market in the United States dropped heavily for a year or so, "God's

A tug of war, March 1924: 'Merry Widows' v. 'The Widowers'.

Waiting Room" became rather empty and we had to take her out.'

To save cruising a new idea of flying passengers to their ports of embarkation was the next logical step and Cunard was well in the forefront here as a new relationship grew up between cruise lines and airlines. This was followed by the 'sail and stay' package holidays – joint cruises and hotel holidays all included in the cruise price.

On September 20th, 1967, the super-cruise-and-Atlantic-express ship of the century first showed herself to the public, as Her Majesty Queen Elizabeth stepped forward on the launching platform at Upper Clyde Shipbuilders, with contract No. 736 towering above her, and announced: 'I name this ship *Queen Elizabeth The Second*. May God Bless her and all who sail in her.'

The giant hull slipped into the Clyde, not only as a new Atlantic challenger, but as a future money-making floating resort. The new Cunard wonder ship was aimed at people who had already become dehumanized by regimented air travel, and wanted to escape to a body and mind-restoring form of journeying around the world. No one knew if it was really going to work. They could only hope; Cunard had to go further – they had to pray. Within an hour of the launch, Cunard offices in London, Southampton and Liverpool received 500 telephone calls congratulating them on the choice of the ship's name which had only been known by four people, the Queen herself, Sir Basil Smallpeice, Sir Michael Adeane, the Queen's private secretary, and Mr Ronald Senior, the deputy chairman.

As usual there had been much speculation as to the name to be chosen and the *Daily Mirror* columnist, 'Cassandra' (Bill Connor, later to become Sir William Connor), wrote in his inimitable way before the launching:

> The next question for romanticists such as myself is to speculate on what they are going to call the new maritime giant, which is known simply as No. 736. I predict there will be enormous pressure to christen the new Cunarder a queen. But which Queen?
>
> We are short of reigning queens in English history. The Normans, the Plantagenets, the Tudors, the Stuarts, the Hanoverians, the Saxe-Coburgs, and the Windsors, have only provided half-a-dozen in the past thousand years.
>
> Two Marys, two Elizabeths, one Anne and one Victoria. Queen Anne was a colourless nobody and Queen Victoria was a colourful somebody.
>
> So R.M.S. *Queen Victoria* is a distinct possibility for that dumpy little old lady was a real character who ruled for 64 years at the height of British imperial wealth and power.
>
> The Americans who will be the main clients for the ship would, I am sure, settle for R.M.S. *Churchill*. They are fond of that old Anglo-American party.
>
> My own suggestion doesn't stand a hope in high water. It is that the new ship be called *John Brown*. A fine solid British name that any commoner should be proud of.
>
> Nobody would know which John Brown. The chap who founded the firm that built the ship. The whisky-drinking Scottish ghillie who for nineteen years dominated Queen Victoria. The John Brown whose soul goes marching on. John Brown the celebrated Northumberland poet. John Brown who wrote the famous dictionary of the Bible. John Brown the celebrated Edinburgh theologian, or any of the 38 John Browns who are listed in the London telephone directory.
>
> It would provide endless argument as to which John Brown was meant, that would rage in every bar in the country, including the bars abroad. R.M.S. *John Brown*. I just wanted to be helpful.

After the launching, Sir Basil Smallpeice commented: 'The *Queen Elizabeth* is nothing if not the product of change, a blending of new ideas and practice in order to meet the challenge of new circumstances. The Queen was moved at the continuance of the tradition of naming Great Cunarders after royal personages. The *Queen Mary* after her grandmother; the *Queen Elizabeth* after her mother; and now this magnificent ship after herself.'

R.M.S. *John Brown* had lost out. But the *Daily Mail* gave their readers the best laugh out of the launching with a cartoon depicting Prime Minister Harold Wilson, slung from a cradle at the bows of the liner, busily painting the name '*King Harold*'!

Hardly had the *Queen Elizabeth 2* reached the fitting-out basin when 171

'Anyone for tennis, Dennis?'
'Wait until I've finished my
morning soup.'

Cunard announced losses of £2 million over a period of six months; three more passenger liners, the *Caronia*, *Carinthia* and *Sylvania*, were to be sold to raise money; and about 2,000 staff dismissed. And this was in spite of the fact that the government, on the eve of the launch, had loaned the company a further £6 million to meet increased costs of materials and wage rates. Every penny of the loan was needed, however, to make the *QE 2* the ultimate super-liner of the twentieth century and get her to sea with full loads of passengers to help start paying dividends on the £30 million Cunard had invested in her. The ship was to have the first computer of its kind in a merchant ship and its costly and sophisticated operational functions would include data logging, alarm scanning, machinery control, prediction of fresh water needs, weather forecasts and control of food stocks.

And among the *QE 2*'s mammoth inventory would be 25 miles of wool carpet, 2 million square feet of Formica laminate, 115 vacuum cleaners, 64 carpet cleaners, 11 baggage and store trucks, 1,300 telephones and 7,440 feet of mooring rope. To give everyone aboard the best possible views there were to be 1,350 port holes and 577 windows from the 13 decks. She was to be supplied with 64,000 items of crockery, 51,000 items of glassware, 35,850 pieces of cutlery, 5,864 tablecloths, 8,600 blankets, 23,000 pairs of sheets, 26,200 pillow slips, 31,000 hand towels, 26,000 bath towels, 1,500 deck rugs and 14,000 glass-towels.

Cunard cash also went in another direction by what was known on Clydebank as 'squirrelling' – stealing from ships being built. Some dishonest workers believed that the more you stole from a ship, the more time it took to complete, and that way you kept a well paid job longer. When Glasgow police searched the home of one *QE 2* worker they found he had taken from the ship in 3 months 30 yards of carpet, 2 chests of drawers, a wall cabinet, 3 bookcases, 3 lounge stools, 4 settee backs, 1 toilet seat, 5 lampshades, 1 bulkhead lamp, an electric radiator, 180 feet of fibreglass, 8 gallons of paint, 6 tea cups and saucers, 6 side plates, 6 cereal plates, 3 cushions, 5 curtains, 2 sheets, a blanket and 350 feet of electric cable. When the man was charged his solicitor told the court: 'He just walked off the ship with the stuff!'

And the day after two new lifeboats were delivered to the *QE 2* they were found to be stripped of their compasses, sirens, torches, rope ladders and iron rations.

Everything depended on the *QE 2* being a success, and shortly before she came into service in 1969, the Cunard Line's new managing director, Mr F.J. Whitworth, made the best of all the adversity by declaring:

'This is *Queen Elizabeth Two* year – the most flexible and sophisticated ship ever to come into service. She represents a complete transformation in Cunard thought.

'We are not decanting old wines into new bottles, but ruthlessly transforming our image from the 'aspidistra and public bar' image which the dear old ships have carried around since 1840. We are getting rid of the images of "dukes and duchesses" on the one hand, and the "Knees Up, Mother Brown" type on the other. We want something more sophisticated but still retaining the Cunard tradition with the same high standards. The *Queen Elizabeth Two* is something new and exciting for the holiday market, not only of today but of tomorrow.'

Some £3 million had been spent on the design of the interior and exterior

Blind man's bottle race.

(*Left*) The Queen's Room on the *QE2*. The ship represented a complete transformation in Cunard thought.

(*Below*) The Queen Mary suite in the *QE2*.

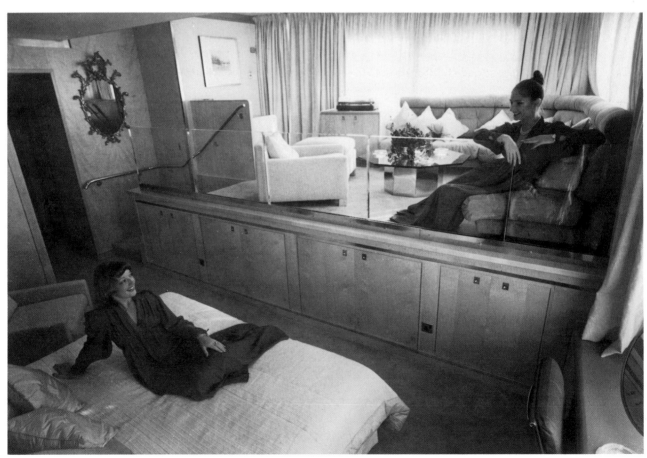

of the *QE 2* and the work had been taken over by a design team headed by James Gardner and Dennis Lennon as joint design co-ordinators, and Cunard's naval architect, Dan Wallace. When the work was completed in February 1968, Cunard organized an exhibition of the interior design and *The Times* commented: 'The impression is of good 1960's hotel design compared with the good 1930's design of the old Queens. Moulded wood, wrought metal, folkweave, and damask are out; plastic, tweed, leather, are in; green, brown and gold are out; oatmeal, sun yellow, dark blue, and magnolia, are in.'

James Gardner, the designer responsible for the outward appearance of the *QE 2*, summed up his intentions for the ship's design.

'We designed to give the passenger a sense of being in a special place, of pleasure and of dignity,' he said. 'The shape of each space already had character, so we clad it in hard and soft texture, tone and colour, to give a variety of atmosphere; quiet, cool, gay; here restrained elegance, there formal simplicity. One atmosphere for night, another for day.'

Spanning two levels and linked by a 24-foot wide spiral staircase, the Double Down Room is the largest of the public rooms. Bedecked in red, gold and glass, the Double Down Room sets a stage of pure drama. The lower level contains a lounge area, bar and dance floor, while the second level accommodates a shopping arcade reminiscent of Houston's famous Galleria in Texas, U.S., as well as a balcony overlooking the dance floor.

The Queen's Room, a light and airy garden lounge, is the other main public room. Passengers are graciously greeted by a bust of her Majesty, Queen Elizabeth II, at the entrance to this sunny room. With soothing shades of blond, white and honey, the decor creates a conducive ambience for the varied and pleasant daily daytime activities which range from yoga to flower arranging. As evening descends, she is transformed into a night club complete with dancing and sophisticated entertainment.

With dancing and music continuing into the early hours, the Theatre Bar is a late night lively spot, and, remodelled in 1985, the Players Club Casino is operated at sea by London Clubs. Equipped with roulette, blackjack and slot machines, the casino even has its own bar. The Magradome, a sliding steel-and-glass canopy, was added over the outdoor pool to convert it into a room by day and night. Two personal royal standards, presented to the ship by Her Majesty Queen Elizabeth the Queen Mother, and Her Majesty Queen Elizabeth II, hang in the stair lobby between the Theatre Bar and Casino.

The *Queen*'s state rooms were designed with spaciousness and luxury being the top priorities. All state rooms have wall-to-wall carpeting; firm and comfortable beds; bath, shower or both; individual climate control; a six-channel radio; and a telephone. Perhaps what add greatly to the *Queen*'s distinction of being the world's ultimate in seagoing luxury are her penthouse suites, the Queen Mary and Queen Elizabeth. Both are situated above and behind the bridge allowing for superb sea views from picture windows and patios. Each suite has two bedrooms, a sitting room, two bathrooms, two patios, and a walk-in wardrobe dressing room. Split level above a bedroom is the sitting room. An elegant yet exceptionally comfortable 12-foot suede sofa, glass-and-satin stainless steel coffee tables, and chairs covered in handmade Scottish tweed comprise the inviting furnishings of these beautiful rooms.

The bedroom decor is equally interesting. Muted beiges and pastel silk convey a sense of grace, ease and comfort with handmade sycamore chests specially designed for the *QE 2*. The carpeted bathrooms have two marble basins, gold-plated fittings, large bathtub shower, bidet and mirrored walls.

The *Daily Telegraph* said: 'There's nothing of the old Lady about the new *Queen Elizabeth Two*. She is smart, crisp and modern, using new colours, fabrics and materials.'

The *Daily Mirror* said: 'She's a swinging super-ship, controversially beautiful . . . Britain's finest . . . She has a regal beauty all her own. It's there for all to see, built into her smooth and simple, sleek and graceful lines. A ship surely to stir the heart of a maritime nation. And one that could be a splendid British enterprise that will pay off in hard cash. That, at least, is the dream. But can she earn money for Cunard who lost £14,000,000 on passenger lines in five years?'

And the man responsible for the interior design, Dennis Lennon, whose previous commissions had included the Cumberland Hotel, London, opera sets and 32 London Steak Houses for J. Lyons and Co., described the result as a 'shippy feel', essential to enjoy the unique experience unobtainable in any other form of travel. 'We have designed the interior to look and feel like a ship,' he explained. 'Not something evocative of an hotel, another liner, or a baronial hall.'

The Cunard publicists working on future trans-Atlantic and cruise brochures for the *QE 2* were already busy preparing words and pictures that asked by what other means of travel one could sit down to an international show in a 530-seat theatre; dance in a two-storey ballroom; eat in one of four luxurious restaurants; make merry in seven bars, two night clubs, and a casino; exercise in one of four swimming pools and a health spa; enjoy Turkish and sauna baths. Add that the ship had apartments for 2,025 people, drive-on/drive-off facilities for eighty cars, together with a hospital and a dental surgery, and it spelt the *QE 2*.

But before *Fielding's Guide* could come out with the description of the *QE 2* as 'a veritable city at sea', Cunard was involved in another revolutionary event to occupy the minds of all those hard at work trying to save the company from sailing into a sea of red ink. It was known as the container ship revolution.

CHAPTER THIRTEEN

The Great Cargo Revolution

Cargo of every description has been transported around the world by Cunard ships ever since *Britannia* sailed on her first voyage across the Atlantic with her holds packed. The cargo business, less spectacular than the passenger side and less well known, has always played an important part in the topsy-turvy finances of the company, and by the 1960s, apart from the three passenger ships left after rationalization had died down, the Cunard group owned some sixty cargo ships operating to the east coast of North America, to India and Pakistan, Australia and New Zealand, the Mediterranean, the Red Sea and Ceylon; India to the U.S. Gulf, and the east coast of North America and the U.S. Gulf to U.K.

They carried everything – petroleum, lubricants, chemicals, iron and steel, cars, textiles, whisky, tobacco, minerals, fertilizers, molasses, cattle, sheep, horses, animal and vegetable oil, tea, wool, jute, bicycles, machinery and transport equipment, electrical goods, timber, refrigerated meats and fruits . . . there was little Cunard did not carry.

Then in the mid-1960s came a technological revolution called 'containerization', which was to shake the shipping world. Before 1965 cargo services had contributed some 60 per cent of Cunard's annual operating revenue during good times, but in 1966 the Port Line made their first loss and there was a deficit on all cargo services of some £300,000, compared with a profit of £1.6 million the year before. Much of this loss was due in part to a long drought in Australia and the resultant drop in agricultural exports, and labour strikes.

Brocklebanks also experienced flagging fortunes at this time trying to maintain its position in the Indian and Pakistan trades, mainly due to the insistence of both India and Pakistan that they carry at least half of their trade in their own ships.

On the other hand, H.E. Moss and Company Tankers Ltd, owners of three 19,000-ton tankers and acquired by Cunard in 1964 and put under the management of Brocklebanks, continued to make a steady profit, and two new ships, products-carriers of 22,000 tons each, were added to the fleet in 1968.

Containerization, as great a change for shipping as the replacement of sail by steam in the mid-nineteenth century, could not have come at a worse time for Cunard. A great deal of money was needed to implement the change and their cargo ship operations had suddenly plunged into the red.

Containerization can be best described as the cheap mechanical *177*

transfer of thousands of individual packages in large containers which can be carried in a ship's hold, or on deck. The idea was to cut down manual dock labour with all its industrial troubles; eliminate pilferage which was widespread in many docks; reduce ship turn-round time in ports; and reduce crews for the new-style carriers. It was also to mean a marked change in the nature of a seaman's employment. A round trip to Australia was to take only about 70 days compared with 160 or more for a conventional cargo ship. And with only 16 hours scheduled for each turn-round, seagoing staff would have to spend virtually all their time aboard. There were to be fewer ports of call and little if any time for crews

to go ashore.

For centuries, methods of loading and unloading ships in dockyards had gone on unchanged, much of it done by manual labour, and there was a great deal of wasted time and money. The containerization revolution started in the United States in 1960 when the Matson Line, running pineapples from San Francisco to Hawaii, first began to use containers stowed on decks of ships.

Then Malcolm McLean, a successful American trucker, whose business was to bring cargo by truck to New York for onward transmission to Puerto Rico, developed the idea of containerization. Dissatisfied and unhappy at the way in which ships were loaded and unloaded in the past, McLean formed the company Sealand and bought and converted a number of tankers to make them capable of rapidly loading and unloading 35-foot containers carried on his trucks. He acquired some dockside land at Port Newark and designed a different kind of terminal which gave ample room for cargo to be properly assembled and moved about on wheels.

The revolution had started and soon shipping companies in many parts of the world were following America's lead. In Britain, four major shipping lines, P. and O., Ocean Steamship, British and Commonwealth and Furness Withy, came together and formed O.C.L. (Overseas Containers Limited) in 1965. Cunard and the Blue Star Line attempted to jump on the band wagon with the argument that this new development should include all lines in the trade. They were turned down by the group and the Cunard board believed that the four O.C.L. lines were then determined to dominate the British cargo trade and leave the rest of them to fade into obscurity.

Cunard decided to bide their time and, like Samuel Cunard, learn first from the mistakes of others before going into the business with carefully planned deliberation. They began by adapting conventional cargo ships to take containers, then experimented in container design in different materials. Philip Bates, who by 1962 had become deputy chairman of Brocklebanks, and, in 1965, the managing director of Cunard Line, explained: 'At this time, on our side of the Atlantic, containerization was regarded as a hedge – no one really knew if it would take off.'

A report put before the Cunard board in 1966 read:

Containerization is not an end in itself; it is, if it is anything, a way of enabling the shipowner to make more money and to service his customers better. We know that full containerization can give enormous savings in handling costs and ships' turn-round times. We also know that the capital required is high and that there are enormous related problems that would have to be solved. Can we obtain some or all of the benefits of containerization without going the whole way? Or, to put it another way, can we devise a system of partial containerization of our trade that will be more profitable to us than either our present system or full containerization?'

One thing was for sure. Cunard did not have the money available to go it   *179* alone. But, when a review of the U.K. Shipping Industry forecast that by 1980 about 80 per cent of all cargo shipped would be containerized, a start had to be made and it could only be done by joining others – partly because of the huge investment and partly to minimize competition.

One of the first consortia joined by Cunard was Associated Container Transportation (Australia) Limited (A.C.T.A.), which planned to operate on the UK/Australia route. In this Cunard had a $42\frac{1}{2}$ per cent interest through its Port Line subsidiary. A.C.T.A. was part of the all embracing container consortium, Associated Container Transportation Limited (A.C.T.), the partners being Ben Line Steamers, Blue Star Line, Ellerman Lines and Thos. and Jas. Harrison, in addition to Cunard.

Then, to containerize the North Atlantic routes, Cunard joined Atlantic Container Line (A.C.L.), a consortium with Swedish, Dutch and French owners, and in 1968, Philip Bates became the consortium's operating company chairman, holding together a company comprising four different nationalities; throughout the container revolution he had been a leading figure and an architect of many developments. When he retired 17 years later this brought to an end the 143-year-old Bates family association with the shipping world.

With a new roll on/roll off service, Atlantic Container Line had started with container ships five times as big, and half as fast again as conventional vessels previously operating on the North Atlantic. Each had a capacity to take 600 containers in holds and on deck, plus the facility to take 200 more if required by the roll on/roll off methods. Each ship could also carry general cargo on trailers and up to a thousand cars. With television 'eyes' to oversee the operation, 600 tons of cargo could be loaded and discharged in an hour and ships turned round in less than a day.

Chairman Sir Basil Smallpeice was well satisfied. 'I was now more than glad that P. and O. and Ocean Steamship, who had thought we were fit only for breaking up, had spurned my original merger offer,' he proclaimed. 'With the Cunard group about to stop losing money on passenger ships, and the whole business back in profit, the long term prospects are exhilarating.'

Three new refrigerated container ships – the equivalent of 18 conventional ships – were ordered to be built for A.C.T.A. by the German shipyard, Bremer-Vulkan, as the British yards, unfortunately, could not match the necessary delivery date. And an order for two A.C.L. container ships, augmenting the Swedish and Dutch ships, was placed with Swan Hunter and later to be named *Atlantic Causeway* and *Atlantic Conveyor*.

In 1968, Blue Star Port Line (Management) Ltd was formed to manage the conventional cargo ships of both Blue Star and Port Line. Meanwhile, Cunard's freight services were put together under one management together with Moss Tankers, becoming known as Cunard-Brocklebank, a company headed by T.H. (Tommy) Telford as managing director. Three years later, on Tommy Telford's retirement, W.B. (Bill) Slater, who had joined Cunard soon after the Second World War having been a captain in the Royal Marines, serving in the 3rd Commando Brigade, was appointed

M.V. *Mahout*, a Brocklebank ship serving the Indian trade.

managing director of Cunard–Brocklebank.

'Port Line and Brocklebank staff always felt that Cunard would be much better concentrating on the passenger side of the business, and allowing them to manage the cargo interests,' Bill Slater explained. 'But from 1955 onwards Cunard got it into their heads that the passenger business was becoming questionable because of the threat from the airlines. This was at the time when one of Cunard's management consultants suggested the company should get out of the passenger business because there was no future in it. As a result Cunard really began to think they should start to make bigger inroads into the cargo business.

'By 1968, Basil Smallpeice had become chairman of Cunard–Brocklebank, Philip Bates was deputy-chairman, Tommy Telford was managing director, and I became operations director.

'For me this involved closing down the cargo side of the Cunard office in New York and appointing an agent. It was by then fully realized that it was only a question of time before we stopped running conventional cargo ships on the North Atlantic.

'Cargo services were gradually withdrawn and container services took over with the building of the *Atlantic Causeway* and the first *Atlantic Conveyor* in 1970; it was the end of general cargo ships on the North Atlantic for Cunard. We tried to hang on as long as we could but in the end they had to go, and Cunard–Brocklebank became the general agency for Atlantic Container Line (A.C.L.) in the U.K.'

By the early 1970s most of the profit was derived from the cargo services *181*

of Cunard, also from Port Line and Brocklebanks, together with the
container consortia operations, the products-carriers of Moss Tankers,
and a new subsidiary, Offshore Marine, a company operating supply boats
serving oil rigs in various parts of the world.

By 1972 the overall management of Port Line was assumed by Cunard–
Brocklebank; in 1976 ten refrigerated fruit ships were acquired from
Maritime Fruit Carriers to introduce Cunard into an even wider type of
cargo operation.

Both Port Line and Brocklebanks, acquired by Cunard during, and immediately after the First World War, had played an important part in the
cargo and freight side of Cunard's history, their ships sailing to the far
corners of the world.

The firm of Thos. and Jno. Brocklebank, accepted as being the oldest
known deep-sea shipping company in the world, traces its origins back to
1741. Daniel Brocklebank, the son of the rector of a village in Cumberland
and apprenticed at an early age to a shipyard at the north west port of
Whitehaven, had, like Samuel Cunard, one ambition in life – to own a
fleet of ships. At the age of 29, married to a Whitehaven girl, Daniel
Brocklebank emigrated to Sheepscutt, Boston, Massachusetts, taking
with him a group of Whitehaven carpenters and seamen.

At Sheepscutt he established his first shipbuilding yard, and in the first
five years built five ships. But in 1775 he had to make a hurried departure in
his fifth built ship, the *Castor*, leaving behind his shipyard, timber and
stores. Massachusetts had overnight become no place for an Englishman
after open insurrection followed the Boston Tea Party. Daniel Brocklebank sailed the *Castor* back to England, found his father and mother had
died during his absence, and sailed off again, this time to Newfoundland.

For the next few years, Captain Brocklebank and the *Castor* turned up
in various parts of the world, trading in the West Indies, crossing
the Atlantic, until finally the *Castor* was lost off Jamaica while being
chased by a privateer. The captain survived and four years later Daniel
Brocklebank sailed back to Whitehaven to start a shipbuilding yard in
England. By the time he died at his Whitehaven home in 1801 he had built
twenty-six ships. His brothers, Thomas and Jonathan, took over the firm
and in 1819, Thomas moved his headquarters to Liverpool while Jonathan
remained in Whitehaven, and for a number of years the firm was divided,
ships being built in Cumberland, registered in Liverpool and sailed from
the Mersey. It wasn't long before Thos. and Jno. Brocklebank became one
of the most important shipping companies on the Mersey, growing in size
and importance ever since.

Port Line was registered in 1914 under the name of the Commonwealth
and Dominion Line Ltd, and was an amalgamation of four family
concerns – Tyser and Company; part of the Star Line of James P. Corry and
Company; part of the Indra Line of T.B. Royden and Company; and the
Anglo-Australian Steam Navigation Company of William Milburn and
Company. It became engaged in the refrigerated and general cargo trades

S.S. *ACT 6*, one of Port Line's refrigerated container ships serving Australasia.

between the U.K. and Australia/New Zealand, and also between the east coast of North America and Australia/New Zealand.

Two years after the line was formed it was decided to name all ships of the fleet after ports in Australia and New Zealand, but it wasn't until 1937 that the official change of name of the company to 'Port Line' was made. Within eight months of the formation of the Commonwealth and Dominion Line, war broke out and midway through the war, in 1916, the directors entered into an agreement with the Cunard Steam-Ship Company whereby Cunard took over all the shares in exchange for Cunard shares and debentures, together with some War Loan and cash.

Sir Alfred Booth and Sir Percy Bates, both Cunard directors, joined the board, whose chairman, W.P. Tyser, vice-chairman, C.T. Milburn, and Sir William Corry became directors of Cunard.

Over the years Port Line has carried every conceivable piece of cargo and freight, including zoo animals, race horses and polo ponies, many for breeding purposes; houses and buildings in Britain have been taken down brick by brick and shipped across the world; Donald Campbell's famous racing car 'Bluebird' came from Australia to Liverpool stowed on deck; over a five-year period, a number of company ships carried a major proportion of the steelwork of Sydney Harbour bridge, and the first experimental shipments of chilled beef from Australia and New Zealand were shipped to Europe by Port Line.

One of the most interesting cargoes was the cottage built in 1755 at Great Ayton, Yorkshire, home of Captain James Cook, the great navigator and discoverer of Australia. The government had the cottage dismantled and shipped in 300 wooden cases in the *Port Dunedin* 12,000 miles to Melbourne for re-erection in time for the City of Melbourne's Centenary Celebrations in 1934.

In 1962 a small zoo was brought into Liverpool in *Port Launceston* from Adelaide for the Dudley Zoological Society in Worcestershire. It included two female kangaroos, two wallabies, six pairs of galahs, one pair of cockatoos, four keas (natives of New Zealand), and one pair of kookaburras (the laughing jackass).

And way back in the nineteenth century one of the first Royden steamers taken over by Port Line was carrying zoological specimens from the Far East for a New York zoo when the cargo broke adrift in a gale and many of the animals, including a Bengal tiger and a large python, got loose and began roaming the deck. All the crew took fright and locked themselves in cabins. Eventually the tiger and the python battled together on the deck. When the fight was over the crew emerged to discover the victor, the python, engaged in eating the tiger.

By 1970, Cunard's financial position had performed another somersault and accountants warned that the company would be £2 million in the red on its operations. Cunard wasn't alone in having to face up to a loss of profits at the time as the whole shipping world was affected. But what worried the Cunard board most of all was that the company could now be 183 ripe for a takeover.

On June 29th, 1971, a bid seemed imminent when there was a sudden upsurge in Cunard share prices on the Stock Exchange and the following day, Trafalgar House Investments Ltd put in a bid which valued Cunard shares around £1.85. Trafalgar House, headed by Nigel Broackes (knighted in 1984), then controlled some 260 subsidiary companies engaged in a wide variety of activities including property and investment, contracting, civil engineering, mining and specialist undertakings, housebuilding, hotel ownership and management, industrial and general activities. It wasn't all that surprising that doubts were expressed as to whether an organization with so wide a range of interests could operate shipping services profitably.

The Cunard board delayed accepting the bid and by the end of July, Nigel Broackes increased Trafalgar's offer to £2.10 per share, and Cunard was not in a financial position to fight off Trafalgar's approach any longer. In true *Dynasty* and *Dallas* fashion the two principals of this behind-the-scenes drama, the young London business tycoon Nigel Broackes and Sir Basil Smallpeice met secretly in a suite of the Hotel Negresco overlooking the Promenade des Anglais at Nice.

Nigel Broackes described the meeting thus:

'He (Sir Basil Smallpeice) had a portfolio of threats combined with inducements for a better price; I added a few pennies per share, and we shook hands . . . I drove Basil on to La Violetta for lunch with Joyce (Mrs Broackes) and our three children, and then back to Nice airport where he collected his Hawker Siddeley HS 125 and flew back to London. I wrote the memorandum of our agreement in pencil on a notepad, we both initialled it, and Basil took it with him to get it typed. I was absolutely thrilled with the acquisition.'

In August 1971, Cunard was officially taken over at a cost of £26 million and acquired assets of £39 million. A reorganization of Cunard within the Trafalgar House group took place immediately, with shipping, hotels and leisure placed together in one division, and the old Cunard board dismissed and replaced from within the new group.

Five months after the takeover, Sir Basil Smallpeice, in his own words, 'let myself quietly over the side and went ashore.'

Shortly after Trafalgar House took control, Nigel Broackes, back in London, paid his first visit to see the major prize his company had won in the takeover deal – the QE 2 at Southampton docks. He was accompanied by Victor Matthews, deputy chairman and managing director of Trafalgar House, who became Lord Matthews of Southgate in 1980, and retired from the Trafalgar board in 1985 after resigning as chairman of Fleet Holdings.

Referring to seeing the QE 2 for the first time since the takeover, Nigel Broackes wrote: 'She had been built with the help of Government loans (not subsidies) at a cost of £33 million, and already the replacement cost would have been over £100 million though she was only two years old.

S.S. *Atlantic Causeway*, Cunard's first roll-on/roll-off container ship built for A.C.L.'s North Atlantic trade.

There would probably never be another, and it was vital to Trafalgar's reputation that the operation of this ship should be a success.'

The takeover of Cunard had shaken the shipping world and after the first shock waves began to settle it became known that Trafalgar House were not the only ones to have been after the company. In the early 1960s, Charles Clore, the financier, and Jack Cotton, the property developer, wanted to make a bid but were stopped by some of their major shareholders. At the same time, P. and O. had made indications that they would like to make an offer but were told in no uncertain terms that this would never be acceptable to Cunard. By the time Trafalgar House made their bid there was no one else in the running. It could not have been better timed.

The last of the famous Bates family to have been associated with Cunard at the top, Philip Bates, in retrospect considers that the Trafalgar House takeover was for the best. Living in retirement in Hampshire, Philip Bates put it this way:

'There was nothing the board could do to prevent the takeover, and the end result has been extremely beneficial for both sides. Looking back into the past, and looking into the future, if a company produces something that is of interest to holidaying people, they will tend to accept it, take it, and pay for it.

'At the higher end of the market there must be long term and continuing interest in sea travel as opposed to Concorde, rocket or space travel.'

Yet, if the critics of the takeover were to be proved right, a great deal still depended on Trafalgar's prize requisite, the *QE 2*, and she still had to prove her worth in the troubled waters of her trade.

The *Cunard Princess* cruises
to places as far apart as
Alaska and Mexico.

CHAPTER FOURTEEN

Cunard Sails on: into the 21st Century

Apart from an uproarious reception in New York to mark her maiden voyage in 1969, the new 'star' of the Cunard Line, and flagship of a nation, the *QE 2*, did not get off to a very good start. The world's fastest passenger ship – the most powerful twin-screw merchant ship afloat; the largest liner with the ability to sail through the Panama and Suez Canal; the ship with a £100,000 computer system, the most sophisticated ever built for a sea-going vessel – developed engine trouble.

In the first year, the wonder ship achieved the most unwelcome notoriety, with headlines in newspapers all over the world, because of serious problems with her turbines. Then, in May 1972, with the turbine problem well behind her, the liner ran into another unwanted situation which made more worldwide headlines. Two days out in the Atlantic from New York, eastbound to Southampton, Captain W.J. 'Bill' Law and Chief Officer 'Bob' Arnott, were handed a de-coded signal from Cunard's London office which read:

THREAT OF EXPLOSION TO DESTROY SHIP UNLESS DEMAND CASH PAYMENT MET. EXPLOSIVES SET ON SIX SEPARATE DECKS. AUTHORITIES ADVISE TAKE ALL NECESSARY PRECAUTIONS. TWO ACCOMPLICES MAY BE ON BOARD. MONITOR ALL CABLES, TELEPHONE MESSAGES.

Shortly before the signal was received in the *QE 2*'s radio room a man had phoned Cunard's New York headquarter's office at 555 Fifth Avenue and told the company's American vice-president, Charles S. Dickson: 'Pay me 350,000 dollars or the *QE 2* will be blasted out of the sea.'

The caller added that he had two accomplices in the liner. One, an ex-convict, the other, a terminal cancer victim. They had instructions to detonate six bombs hidden in bulkheads, and both men were ready to die if the money wasn't paid. Further instructions would be sent to Cunard by the caller.

Cunard in New York called in the F.B.I. and in Britain Scotland Yard and the Ministry of Defence went into immediate action. Within a very short time an R.A.F. Nimrod reconnaissance aircraft had taken off from St Mawgan in Cornwall to advise on sea and weather conditions for a proposed air drop of four bomb disposal experts over the *QE 2*, and to act as a communications centre between the threatened liner and police and defence experts in Britain.

Meanwhile, a hunt was started throughout the *QE 2* for the bombs and   *187* the two men answering descriptions of the ex-convict and cancer victim, and Captain Law broadcast the following announcement to all passengers:

'We have received information concerning the threat of a bomb explosion on board this ship sometime during the voyage. We have received such threats in the past which have all turned out to be hoaxes. However, we always take them seriously and take every possible precaution. This time we are being assisted by the British Government who are sending out bomb disposal experts. They will be parachuted into the sea, picked up by boat, and brought on board.'

There was no panic. The Nimrod found the *QE 2* 750 miles east of Cape Race, Newfoundland. Ninety minutes later, a Royal Air Force Hercules came through low cloud over the *QE 2*, bang on target, and a resounding cheer went up from passengers crowding the decks, many of them having spent anxious hours making bets amongst themselves on the time outside help would take to arrive.

The cheers had hardly died down when two figures in black frogmen suits on the ends of parachutes came swinging down through the cloud level, and Sergeant Clifford Oliver of the S.A.S. and Corporal Thomas Jones of the British Special Boat Service, both carrying heavy loads of equipment, hit the sea only 200 yards ahead of the *QE 2*'s bows. A second pass by the aircraft followed and Lieutenant Richard Clifford of the Royal Marines, and Captain Robert Williams of the Royal Army Ordnance Corps, parachuted into the sea. For Captain Williams it was his first parachute jump.

The following afternoon a message was delivered to the Cunard offices in New York ordering Charles Dickson to take 350,000 dollars to a phone booth in New York, and await a call. Charles Dickson set off with the cash and entered the phone booth. As the phone rang the voice at the other end, which he immediately recognized, asked: 'Why have you brought in the law?' Mr Dickson answered that if the F.B.I. hadn't been notified there would have been no money forthcoming from Cunard. He was then given instructions to go to a washroom of a nearby café where there would be a further message taped under a washbasin. The caller warned that two guns would be trained on Mr Dickson the whole time. Mr Dickson did as he was ordered and found the message, which told him to drive over Bear Mountain Bridge to the town of Beacon, and leave the money at a spot in an out-of-town parking lot. Once again, Mr Dickson did as he was told while the F.B.I. kept watch at a discreet distance. All day and night the F.B.I. kept surveillance on the spot where the money had been left but no one came to pick it up and eventually it was returned to Cunard.

Aboard the *QE 2* a thorough search by the bomb disposal experts and crew for bombs failed to find any and when the pay-up-or-else deadline passed, life on the *QE 2* returned to normal, the public radio communications system was re-opened and for the next twenty-four hours was blocked with calls from the world's press, T.V. and radio reporters, and

passengers telling anxious relatives and friends ashore that they were safe.

Months later a man was arrested in New York, charged with extortion, found guilty and sentenced to twenty years in the penitentiary. The F.B.I. were satisfied that there had been no bombs aboard the *QE 2*, no accomplices, and it had all been the work of one lone con-man.

After this rude interruption in the *QE 2*'s early days the great new liner with her beautifully graceful lines and her modern hotel-style interior soon came into her own, won universal praise, and more important for Cunard at the time – made money.

Trafalgar House, the *QE 2*'s new owners, with Nigel Broackes as chairman, Victor Matthews as deputy chairman and managing director, and Eric W. Parker, as group finance director, were confident, given time, that the *QE 2* would be a winner. More money was invested in the ship to ensure that food, services and sales were put in good order; the de luxe penthouses were added in unused space behind the bridge; an extra kitchen was introduced; and every marketing device was used to fill the ship and keep it fully booked with passengers.

In 1974 there was a setback for the Cunard Line when the *Cunard Ambassador*, built in 1972 for the American cruise market, became a total loss following an engine room fire as she was sailing to pick up passengers off Key West in Florida. A beautiful ship which could carry 650 passengers in superb air-conditioned comfort, the *Ambassador* had state rooms all named after famous Cunarders of the past, *Mauretania*, *Aquitania*, *Britannia* and *Carmania*, and the main restaurant, set high in the superstructure, gave panoramic sea views. What was left of the ship after the fire had to be sold off and she ended up as a live sheep carrier.

By 1975, Trafalgar House was able to report to shareholders that despite national and international recession, the *QE 2* had earned the highest profit for several years from a winter round-the-world voyage and a high level of activity on the North Atlantic during the summer. The only remaining cruise ship in the fleet at that time, the *Cunard Adventurer* (sold in 1977) had also sailed virtually full for most of the year.

1976 saw the introduction of two new purpose-built cruise ships, *Cunard Countess* and *Cunard Princess*, and in 1977 the *Cunard Princess* was invested in her title by the late Princess Grace of Monaco in a royal champagne christening in New York. With Cunard container and conventional cargo ships all doing well, Nigel Broackes was able to report: 'Cunard is now a highly important component of the group.' But he also had to tell shareholders that he was not happy with the future outlook for shipping in Britain and warned that the Russians had suddenly become the biggest cruise ship operators in the world with a fleet of more than sixty passenger liners, and had entered on a policy to enfeeble the West through uneconomic competition in both passenger and cargo trades.

At the end of 1978 the 'yo-yo' finances of the shipping world found Cunard's shipping division of Trafalgar House somewhat affected and it was necessary to accept an attractive offer for the entire bulk carrier fleet. The reason for this setback included a weakness in the U.S. dollar, a *189* longshoreman's strike on the U.S. Eastern Seaboard, industrial unrest in Australia, escalating oil prices, and worldwide over capacity, something which later reached enormous proportions.

With continuing worldwide recession and the weakness in the volume of British exports, 1979 was no better, and the situation led to the sale of Transmeridan Air Cargo (acquired in June 1977) in exchange for a 35 per cent holding in British Cargo Airlines, plus the withdrawal of Cunard's Indian Services, together with a sheep-carrying venture which had until then done extremely well.

Unfortunately, British Cargo Airlines fell victim to rapidly escalating prices for aviation fuel, and totally inadequate freight rates, ceasing to trade in 1980. Cunard had, however, in the meantime, taken a two-third interest in a more specialized aircraft operation, and formed Heavy Lift Cargo Airlines, which had acquired the five remaining Belfast freighter aircraft of the R.A.F. with unique cargo capacity; the company progressed by building up new customers who valued the Belfast's capability to carry high volume indivisible items by air all over the world.

Despite reverses, the fortunes of Cunard have proved that those critics who thought the Trafalgar takeover would never work were wrong. By the close of 1983 the *QE 2* had become a profitable venture and Cunard Line achieved record earnings in what had been a difficult year for the industry as a whole. In May of 1983, Cunard had signed contracts to acquire the highly acclaimed luxury motor vessels *Sagafjord* and *Vistafjord* together with the business of their owners, Norwegian American Cruises (N.A.C.). The following year, *Sagafjord* and the *QE 2* were awarded the top qualifications of five plus stars in the 1984 edition of *Fielding's World Wide Cruises*, and the *Cunard Countess* and *Cunard Princess* were increased to four stars each; *Vistafjord* now also has five star rating. And for the second successive year, the *Sagafjord* was voted 'Ship of the Year' by the World Ocean and Cruise Liner Society.

Throughout, and after the Trafalgar takeover, the new organization had been at pains to stress that they were never involved in any so-called 'break-up' situation or financial opportunism, and that they never bought anything they did not intend to integrate into the group. So it was not all that surprising when, in 1976, Trafalgar bought the prestigious and famed Ritz hotel, centrally located in Mayfair, Piccadilly, a stroll from Buckingham Palace, to entice Cunard's richer trans-Atlantic passengers to stay in a top London hotel.

The Ritz, designed and built in 1906 for Swiss-born hotelier, Caesar Ritz, in Louis XVI style, became known as 'the best hotel with the best address in London', but had temporarily fallen on hard times. However, it soon returned to prosperity after the takeover with Cunard's special advantage of being able to market it to the upper sector of the *QE 2* first-class clientele. With 139 superbly appointed rooms and luxury suites, the Ritz today is back as a masterpiece of beautiful marble and classic baroque style.

190   When first opened, it became second home for the landed gentry and a

rendezvous for the crowned heads of Europe. Since then, Queen Elizabeth, the Queen Mother and Princess Margaret have dined on the Ritz's famed cuisine; Prince Charles has danced on a piano played by Elton John at a private party there; the late Lord Mountbatten was a frequent diner; Rex Harrison, Fred Astaire and Sophia Loren have happy memories of the Ritz; and Jackie Onassis once described the hotel as 'Like Heaven'!

New de luxe rooms with 18th-century French marble fireplaces have been added and Cunard guests can now relax in Louis XVI fauteuils in the sitting rooms, while Italian marbles and American cherry woodwork grace the bathrooms. Scottish lace, intricately designed brocade, and flawless silks and taffetas add to the classic decor, while the famous Palm Court has been retained and several popular traditions, like tea dances, classical music, cabaret at dinner and evening fashion shows have been revived.

Nigel Broackes had, without success, been trying to buy the Savoy Hotel, London, for the company, but had also had an eye on The Ritz for some time. Control of The Ritz was in the hands of Sir Guy Bracewell Smith through the Park Lane Hotel Company. Then, one day, Victor Matthews, Trafalgar's deputy chairman, went to The Ritz for lunch and was introduced to Sir Guy.

Sir Guy, the son of a former Lord Mayor of London, was sitting in the Palm Court looking tired and dispirited when the introduction to Victor Matthews was made. At the time he was particularly concerned because The Ritz, which had not been modernized in seventy years, was beginning to look a little tired itself and had not the resources to restore its original magnificence.

Within an hour of the meeting, Victor Matthews was on the phone to Nigel Broackes, who was taking a short winter break with his wife in Barbados.

'We can have it for seven pounds a share,' was all Victor Matthews had to say and without any names being mentioned Nigel Broackes knew what it was all about and agreed to a deal. The Ritz was acquired for £2.7 million in cash.

Extensive improvements carried out by the new owners gained The Ritz the Egon Ronay Award as Hotel of the Year in 1978, and within seven years the hotel was showing record bookings.

At the time The Ritz was acquired, Trafalgar House already owned two hotels in the Caribbean, the Paradise Beach Hotel in Barbados, and the La Toc Hotel, St Lucia, and hoped to further concentrate on the luxury end of the leisure market. In 1985 they added the Stafford Hotel, in St James's, to further complement the de luxe ships operated by the Cunard Line. The Stafford Hotel, a member of the Prestige Hotel Consortium, has historic wine cellars which date back three hundred years, impeccable service, and a club-like atmosphere which goes back to the eighteenth century when the hotel was known as one of London's famous West End clubs, the Stafford Club.

The Cunard Paradise Beach Hotel in Barbados is a 190-room resort *191* located on one of the finest beaches in the Caribbean, and features a variety of accommodation, all with private balconies and spectacular views over the sea, or set in vibrant tropical gardens. The Cunard Hotel La Toc and the La Toc suites comprise an elegant beachfront resort in a private 110-acre valley on the unspoilt island of St Lucia. Cunard offers a week at sea aboard *Cunard Countess* with a week ashore at this hotel which also features round-trip airfares from New York and Miami.

Many of the guests for Cunard's two London hotels arrive in the U.K. today by British Airway's supersonic Concorde, which flies the Atlantic faster than a rifle bullet, linking London and New York (3,500 miles) in little more than three hours. In 1983, Cunard and British Airways came together to introduce special Concorde flights for *QE 2* passengers sailing trans-Atlantic with a popular programme which became known as the SS–ST (Superliner Supersonic Shuttle Travel), sailing one way on the *QE 2*, and flying Concorde the other.

Since then, the *QE 2*/Concorde connection has been hailed on both sides of the Atlantic as a 'perfect marriage' and, in 1985 alone, over 14,000 passengers enjoyed the magical combination available between London and New York, Washington or Miami, together with inaugural Concorde flights for *QE 2* passengers to and from Houston, Detroit, Oklahoma City, Atlanta, Columbus, Cleveland, Colorado Springs, Philadelphia and Pittsburg. In 1986, Louisville, Oakland, Tampa and San Antonio were added to the list for Concorde's maiden visits, and today it is estimated that *QE 2* passengers who fly one way and sail the other account for 75 per cent of British Airways' charter business for its supersonic Concordes.

'It is refreshing that a great passenger liner, whose forebears were made redundant by developing air travel, contributes positively today to both Concorde's success and first trailblazing of new routes,' said Ralph M. Bahna, managing director of Cunard passenger shipping.

Fascinating trivia facts about the *QE 2* came to light during a quiz organized on a Cunard Caribbean cruise in 1985 when most of the passengers appeared to be unaware that since the ship's maiden voyage, the *QE 2* has steamed 1,918,826 miles, equalling 243 trips around the world; that 3 football pitches could be placed along the length of the ship; that it would take 4 months to participate in all *QE 2*'s passenger activities; the ship uses 150 lb. of caviar on every 5-day trans-Atlantic crossing; 10,000 eggs are consumed daily at breakfast; the liner visits about 150 different ports each year; the British actress Hermione Gingold officially opened a branch of Harrods store on *QE 2* in June 1984; the *QE 2* provides 3 million meals annually; the *QE 2* only clears the Panama Canal by 18 inches; Burt Lancaster once 'ran' the full length of *QE 2*'s boat deck on his hands; the *QE 2* was the first western liner allowed into a mainland Chinese port after 1945.

Ralph Bahna spent seven years with Trans World Airlines before joining Cunard in New York in 1973 and it is said of him in the States that he came down out of the skies to help the cruise industry fill its berths through marketing knowhow. Bahna says of the future: 'The amount of creativity we are going to see in the next three to four decades will be staggering. The sea, as part of the travel industry, is like outer space. You can conjure up many uses for land, but we haven't scratched the surface of what we can do with the sea.' He sees ships and air travel complementing each other still further, and he believes the cruise industry has barely tapped the full potential of the market.

'We want to be a top-end company where people are looking for something extra in the leisure business, maritime oriented, but not exclusively,' he added. 'We want to dominate in the quality market in the sea, but also maintain similar quality hotels in those ports to which we sail.

'Cunard is still one of the most forceful names in the United States with regard to passenger ships, and if Americans don't think of Cunard as part of the United States, they certainly think of it as an adopted company.'

Cunard is now continuing with plans to 'expand quickly and aggressively' into luxury hotel management in both Britain and America, and in 1986 they announced that they had been granted a long-term contract to manage the 238-room Watergate Hotel in Washington, the hotel which featured prominently in the infamous Watergate scandal surrounding ex-President Richard Nixon.

Four Cunard ships were despatched to the Falklands war in 1982, which involved the recovery by Britain of the Falkland Islands and South Atlantic Dependencies from invading Argentine forces. The *QE 2*, the *Atlantic Causeway* and the *Saxonia* (III) returned safely, but the *Atlantic Conveyor** which was transporting Harrier Jump Jet aircraft and helicopters was hit by an enemy Exocet missile and sunk with the loss of 12 lives, 6 Cunard men and 6 servicemen.

The missile struck the vessel during an Argentinian air strike on May 25th, causing an intensive fire which eventually burned the ship out. Twenty-eight of the crew and more than 100 servicemen aboard survived. Of the 6 Cunard men who were lost, one, Frank Foulkes, petty officer, engine room, was found drowned, while the remaining five, Captain Ian North, John Benjamin Dobson, petty officer, deck, James Hughes, petty officer, engine room. Ernest Norman Vickers, petty officer, engine room, and David Reginald Stuart Hawkins, steward, were missing, all presumed dead.

Captain North, aged 57, one of the finest masters of Cunard's cargo fleet, had survived two sinkings in the Second World War. Because of his full set

The late Captain Ian North aboard *Atlantic Conveyor* before the ship was sunk off the Falklands.

*In 1984, a second *Atlantic Conveyor*, 820 feet long, incorporating new military defence capabilities following the lessons of the Falklands war, was launched from the Tyneside Wallsend Yard of Swan Hunter by Mrs Michael Heseltine, the wife of the then British Minister of Defence.

of white bushy whiskers and moustache he was affectionately known as 'Captain Bird's Eye'. One of the survivors, Captain Michael Layard, the senior Royal Navy officer aboard the *Atlantic Conveyor* later awarded the C.B.E., was on the bridge with Captain North when the ship was struck. Together they took the decision to abandon ship. 'We left the ship together, the last to go,' said Capt. Layard. 'He, as master, went down the side three steps behind me. I know he got in the water, and I know he got to a raft. But nobody saw him after that.'

Liverpool's Anglican Cathedral, commanding dominant views of the Mersey waterfront, was the fitting setting for a service of remembrance on June 11th, 1982, for those who perished aboard the *Atlantic Conveyor*. The lesson was read by the then chairman of Cunard Lord Matthews and the service was attended by over 2,000 people.

Liverpool was her port of registry, and it was from the Mersey that she had made her maiden voyage on A.C.L.'s north Atlantic service twelve years previously.

On October 11th, 1982, the following awards were made to Cunard personnel for their parts in the Falklands campaign:

Atlantic Conveyor

Distinguished Service Cross (Posthumous): Captain Ian North.

Queen's Gallantry Medal: Third Engineer Brian Williams.

Queen's Commendation for Brave Conduct: PO2 (E) Boleslaw Czarnecki.

Mentioned in Despatches: Chief Officer John Brocklehurst; Chief Engineer James Stewart.

Atlantic Causeway

British Empire Medal: Chief Cook Alan Leonard.

Civil List

Commander of the British Empire: W.B. Slater, in recognition of the part played by Cunard in support of the Falklands campaign.

In addition, three members of the Royal Navy, an R.A.F. Squadron Leader and a Flight Sergeant who were in the *Atlantic Conveyor*, all received awards.

Of Captain Ian North's posthumous award of the Distinguished Service Cross, the citation in the *London Gazette* read:

> On 14th April 1982, SS *Atlantic Conveyor* was laid up in Liverpool. On 25th April she deployed to the South Atlantic converted to operate fixed and rotary wing aircraft and loaded with stores and equipment for the Falkland's Task Force. This astonishing feat was largely due to Captain North's innovation, leadership and inexhaustible energy.

Vistafjord.

SS *Atlantic Conveyor* joined the Carrier Battle Group on 19th May 1982 and was immediately treated as a warship in most respects. Almost comparable in manoeuvrability, flexibility and response, Captain North and the ship came through with flying colours. When the ship was hit on the 25th May, Captain North was a tower of strength during the difficult period of damage assessment leading up to the decision to abandon ship. He left the ship last with enormous dignity and calm and his subsequent death was a blow to all. A brilliant seaman, brave in war, immensely revered and loved, his contribution to the Campaign was enormous and epitomised the great spirit of the Merchant Service.

The citation for the award of the Queen's Gallantry Medal to Third Engineer Officer Brian Williams told how he was on watch in the Engine Control Room of the *Atlantic Conveyor* with a mechanic when the Exocet hit. Hearing the mechanic calling for help, the engineer officer put on breathing apparatus in the smoke-filled control room and set off to the rescue of the mechanic whom he found, trapped and seriously injured following a further large explosion:

> Mr Williams went quickly to get help. Then, realising that a further rescue mission was a forlorn hope and knowing there was grave danger of further explosions and the spread of fire, he armed himself

with asbestos gloves and fresh breathing apparatus and accompanied by the Doctor and a PO Engineer again braved the appalling heat and smoke for a further attempt to rescue the mechanic. However, as they approached, the conditions became literally unbearable and the mission had to be abandoned. Mr Williams made his report calmly and then went to the Breathing Apparatus store where he began valiant efforts to recharge air breathing bottles. He was eventually ordered to the upper deck to abandon ship. Throughout the incident, Mr Williams showed exceptional bravery and leadership and a total disregard for his own safety.

Both the *Atlantic Causeway* and the *Saxonia* (III) went through the thick of the fighting as did the P. and O. liner *Canberra* which transported troops right into the main battle area.

Meanwhile Cunard's civil-registered Belfast aircraft operated magnificently flying supplies to and from Ascension Island, and after the cessation of hostilities Cunard ships carried on 'ferry' work between the U.K. and the Falklands to help keep the 8,000-mile umbilical cord unbroken.

The *QE 2*'s trooping voyage to South Georgia had been remarkable in that she was converted in a period of only eight days at Southampton to carry 3,500 troops of the Fifth Infantry Brigade (the Scots and Welsh Guards and the Gurkha Rifles), fitted with helicopter platforms, military satellite receivers, and equipment to refuel at sea, and sailed unescorted and without air cover to South Georgia where she transferred the troops. She then brought back to Britain 640 survivors of the sunken British warships, H.M.S. *Coventry*, *Antelope* and *Ardent*.

The conversion of the *QE 2* involved seventeen miles of carpeting being covered with fibreboard, panelled walls protected, curtains removed, chairs and five grand pianos taken off, the ship's casino turned into a dormitory, and the Tables of the World and Columbia Restaurants turned into mess halls. Officers took their meals in the Queen's Grill and non-commissioned officers ate in the Princess Grill. *QE 2*'s executive chef, John Bainbridge, who reigned over a staff of 135 and had been with Cunard for over 40 years, saw to it that the Gurkhas were provided with a special curry dish every evening during the 15-day journey to South Georgia.

Chef Bainbridge's grocery list for the *QE 2* generally included quail, caviar, foie gras, smoked pork loins, pheasant, lobster and duck. For the troops on the voyage to the Falklands his kitchens turned out dishes like cream of leek soup, brisket of beef with beans and potatoes, selections of cold meats and salads, apple pie with custard, tea and coffee. There were no complaints.

Captain Peter Jackson, aged sixty, was in command of the *QE 2* during the whole 26-day operation to South Georgia and back. He was accompanied by 640 of his crewmen, all volunteers, and chosen from 1,000 who had volunteered their services.

After the *QE 2*'s return to Southampton, Captain Jackson said: 'Once we got into the hostile area we fitted up a gun emplacement on each wing with two five-inch Browning automatics!' That was the only defence the *QE 2* had, yet it was known that two Argentine submarines were at sea with orders to seek out and sink her. But the Cunard luck, seamanship and speed prevailed, with foul weather, fog, snow, gales and icebergs proving the liner's best defence against the searching enemy. One massive ice field through which Captain Jackson helped to thread the *QE 2* to safety contained more than one hundred icebergs, some of which extended three hundred feet above the water line and measured half a mile in length.

After the Falklands war, it took nine feverish weeks to get the *QE 2* back to its luxury former self to catch up with the last half of the lucrative tourist 'high season'. Most of the seventeen miles of carpeting and Burma teak decking had to be replaced, several of her distinctively chic and majestic rooms completely re-decorated, as well as a number of improvements. The Queen's Grill, once a red and gold room, was re-done in cobalt blue and green silk, with silver trim and polished sycamore. The Casino was expanded and the walls recovered in green leather with gold velvet curtains, and a Golden Door Health Spa was installed with Jacuzzi whirlpool baths. Back came the five grand pianos, half a ton of caviar, 17,000 bottles of champagne and other wines, and a botanical garden of potted plants, together with all other stores, ready for another trip to New York with Captain Jackson very much in command again.

From the end of the Falklands war to 1987, Cunard has concentrated most of its efforts in bringing its famed shipping line back to former glory with the ultimate object of continuing to keep the cargo shipping and aircraft fleet profitable; operating its passenger ships in the top rung of the market; expanding its hotel operations; developing competitively priced cruise package holidays, including free or very low cost air transportation; and continuing to give *QE 2* passengers the opportunity of flying on a British Airways Concorde at far below normal tariff.

The company is working hard to maintain a strong presence in most popular travel regions. In August 1986 it was announced that Cunard had taken over the running of Sea Goddess Cruises, a Norwegian company, including a long-term agreement to operate two small ultra de luxe vessels, *Sea Goddess I* and *Sea Goddess II*, both built like royal yachts and charging passengers £400 a day.

The Sea Goddesses are sleek 340-feet luxury motor yachts which since they came into service in 1984 and 1985 respectively have perfected a concept of all-inclusive luxury cruising at sea in an intimate, private atmosphere, with passengers feeling they are guests on a friend's elegant private yacht where all one's pleasures are attended to with discretion and superb attention to detail. They visit exotic ports of call in Europe, the Caribbean, Alaska, South America and the Java Sea. A casino, swimming pool, gymnasium and sauna are all provided.

Ralph Bahna explained: 'With this acquisition, Cunard will be the world's only cruise operator offering three completely different types of luxury from which to choose, ranging from the superliner *QE 2* to the highly personalised *Sagafjord* and *Vistafjord*, to the private yacht-like cruising of the *Sea Goddesses*. The addition of the *Sea Goddesses* into the Cunard family will help solidify Cunard's pre-eminence at the top end of the luxury cruise market.'

Apart from her regular Atlantic crossings and world cruises, the *QE 2* took part in a special commemorative voyage in May 1986, to mark the 50th anniversary of the *Queen Mary*'s maiden voyage to New York, and on July 3rd, 1986, arrived in New York carrying a replica of the 'Freedom Torch' – Cunard's gift to the American nation for the opening of Liberty Weekend, the national celebration of the centennial of the Statue of Liberty.

In October 1986, the *QE 2* was taken out of service for six months to be effectively re-built in order to extend her life for at least another twenty years. Major renovations included the installation of an all-diesel electric propulsion plant with nine generators, which increases her speed to $32\frac{1}{2}$ knots, thus maintaining her position as the fastest passenger ship afloat. The rejuvenation cost £96 million so that the pride of the world's merchant fleet, and the last of her kind, will sail well into the twenty-first century.

Considering the high cost of the project, Eric Parker, chairman of Cunard, explained that two years of effort and time had been devoted to finding an economic means of extending the life of the *QE 2*.

'I am pleased that Cunard, in the end, was able to justify the decision taken,' he said. 'The eventual withdrawal of the ship from service would have meant the end of modern-day trans-Atlantic sea service and the demise of a vessel which is truly considered the pride of the world's merchant fleet.

'The work will ensure that the *QE 2* will be able to operate competitively for at least another twenty years, avoiding the fate of her royal predecessors, *Queen Elizabeth* and *Queen Mary*.'

So in the year 1987 the last bastion of a mode of travel and a way of life continues, hopefully, into a bright new future and another century, still a source of wonder to both old and young when sighted sailing majestically off coasts throughout the world. Her steam turbine plant has in the refit been replaced by MAN-BMW diesel electric engines which resemble a 92-megawatt power station and will result in substantial savings in both fuel and maintenance. More luxury cabins and further new passenger facilities have been added and there has been modernization of kitchens, passenger cabins and deck areas; the *QE 2* has emerged as the most contemporary ship afloat, the flagship of a fleet of top-rated luxury cruise ships.

To bring the *QE 2* even further up-to-date and to follow other trend-setting additions on board, satellite television has been made possible by the fitting of a 1,100 dish antenna, poised on a gyroscope, together with a TV studio. In July 1986 the first satellite transmission of a TV programme from a merchant ship at sea, using a system conceived by the British company, Ocean Satellite Television, went out from the *QE 2* sailing between Bermuda and New York.

Some 195 passenger ships have been built and acquired to sail under the Cunard flag since 1840, and the advice given by a certain old lady passenger to a friend that 'Cunard always gets you there,' holds good to the present day. Samuel Cunard first conceived the idea of providing a regular and dependable steamship service in 1840. It was his vision that ships could run on schedules like trains. His idea was that ships should sail on specified dates, from specified ports, and arrive on time at specified destinations. It was a historic and monumental concept and not only did Samuel Cunard have the vision but he also had the ability to bring it to fruition and make plans to see that it continued into the future.

Those who have followed have kept to the course he set.

Selected Bibliography

BOOKS

Arnott, Captain Robert Harry, and Ronald L. Smith, *Captain of the Queen* (New English Library, London, 1982)

Bisset, Sir James, KT., C.B.E., *Commodore*, written in collaboration with P.R. Stephenson (Angus and Robertson, London and Australia, 1961)

Broackes, Nigel, *A Growing Concern* (Weidenfeld and Nicolson, London, 1979)

DeLand, Antoinette, *Fielding's World Wide Cruises* (William Morrow, New York, 1986)

Deeson, A.F.L., *An Illustrated History of Steamships* (Spurbooks, Buckinghamshire, 1976)

Grant, Kay, *Samuel Cunard – Pioneer of the Atlantic Steamship* (Abelard–Schuman, New York and London, 1967)

Gibson, John Frederick, *Brocklebanks*, Vol I and II, (Henry Young and Sons, Liverpool, 1953)

Greenhill, Basil, and Ann Giffard, *Travelling by Sea in the 19th Century* (Adam and Charles Black, London, 1972)

Hyde, Francis E., *Cunard and the North Atlantic* (1840–1973) (Macmillan, London, 1975)

Lacey, Robert, *The Queens of the North Atlantic* (Sidgwick and Jackson, London, 1973)

MacDougall, Philip, *Mysteries of the High Seas* (David and Charles, Devon, 1984)

Marr, Commodore Geoffrey, *The Queen and I* (Granada, London, 1973)

Phillips-Birt, Douglas, *When Luxury Went to Sea* (David and Charles, Devon, 1971)

Potter, Neil and Jack Frost, *QE 2* (Harrap, London, 1969)

Poolman, Kenneth, *Armed Merchant Cruisers* (Leo Cooper in association with Secker and Warburg, London, 1985)

Rentell, Philip, *Historic Cunard Liners* (Atlantic Transport Publishers, Cornwall, 1986)

Roche, T.W.E., *Samuel Cunard and the North Atlantic* (Macdonald, London, 1971)

Russell, Captain A.G., *Port Line* (Eyre and Spottiswoode, Kent, 1985)

Staff, Frank, *The Transatlantic Mail* (Granada, London/Adlard Coles, 1956)

Smallpeice, Sir Basil, *Of Comets and Queens* (Airlife Publishing, Shrewsbury, 1981)

Stephens, Leonard A., *The Elizabeth – Passage of a Queen* (Allen and Unwin, London, 1969)

Warwick, Ronald, and William Flayhart, *QE 2* (W.W. Norton, New York and London, 1985)

Ward, Douglas, *Complete Handbook to Cruising* (Berlitz, 1986)

Winter, C.W.R., *Queen Mary – Her Early Years Recalled* (Patrick Stephens, Wellingborough, 1986)

NEWSPAPERS AND PERIODICALS

The files of: *Cunarder Magazine*; *Weekly Illustrated* (Odhams Press); *Ship to Shore* (the publication of the Oceanic Navigation Research Society, California, U.S.A.); *The Shipbuilder* (Benn Brothers Marine Publications); *The Times*; *Daily Telegraph*; *Daily Mail*; *Daily Mirror*; *Liverpool Daily Post*; *Southern Evening Echo*; *Country Life*; *Boston Advertiser*.

Index